LIFE WITH A HOLE IN IT
That's How The Light Gets In

The Wisdom Of An Awakened Heart

Vicki Woodyard

"... shines a bold light on one woman's journey through her husband's diagnosis and death from cancer and into the domain of a fierce wisdom and awakened heart. Ablaze with light!"

Ronda LaRue, Author of *Remembering Who You Really Are* & *The Art of Living Your Destiny!*

BookLocker.com, Inc.
2010

DEDICATION

For my son, Rob

And for all those who appreciate a good
truth when they hear one.

ACKNOWLEDGEMENTS

Jerry Katz, of Nonduality.org has been a friend since the beginning. Thanks, Jerry.

I am also grateful to Dr. Bernie Siegel, who saw something in my writing and inspired me on many different levels.

To Elsa Bailey, a mentor and friend, a believer in all things good.

This book contains many beautiful thoughts of my friend Peter. Thank you, Peter, wherever you are.

To Julia Melges-Brenner, who "saw" this book in its entirety.

To Connie Caldes, *Dream Stories*. Her shamanic journeys feed my spirit.

To all the wonderful cancer patients I have met who have inspired me by their willingness to love and laugh as a way of healing.

To the late John Logan, who taught me many things I needed to know and whose wisest counsel was to "sit down and have some hot chocolate."

And finally, I have my late husband Bob to thank for encouraging me to find my passion. This is it.

PRAISE FOR VICKI WOODYARD'S WRITING

Bernie Siegel, M.D., Author of *Faith, Hope & Healing* and *365 Prescriptions For The Soul*, says, "Vicki is one of those rare souls who can show us all how to turn the charcoal into a diamond through her creativity. Her words can guide us all to a place of healing."

"Vicki's unique voice is honest, direct, spiritually raw." Josh Baran, *The Tao of Now*

"Vicki Woodyard is one of the treasures of spiritual literature." Jerry Katz, Nonduality.com, Editor: *One - Essential Writings on Nonduality*

"Your words are working; I can feel them in my bones." Reader Comment

Ronda La Rue, *Remembering Who You Really Are* and *The Art of Living Your Destiny*! says, "Ablaze with light!"

"This is good reading. It made me smile and laugh. The words are drenched with love and a sense of humor along with reverence and awe for the mystery of life. I recommend this book!" Scott Kiloby, *Reflections of the One Life, Love's Quiet Revolution, Living Realization.*

Elsa Bailey, Concord, CA says, "Your words, always heart-driven, are able to rattle the bars on the mind-cage we all live in."

Chuck Hillig, Author of *Enlightenment for Beginners, Seeds for the Soul, Looking for God: Seeing the Whole in One, The Way*

IT Is, and *The Magic King,* says, "Very readable, life-affirming and filled with deep compassion. Highly recommended."

TABLE OF CONTENTS

FOREWORD

Vicki and I met years ago when we linked websites. It was at a time when few nonduality sites were online, and it was a joy to link up with another being who saw life through a similar lens.

Thus, throughout these years, I've been reading Vicki's unique and luminous writings about her inward journey. More than once, tragedy has been an uninvited guest in her life. Yet her approach to grief is open, frank, heartful, sprinkled with humor. She writes short, pointed pieces, which roll like pearls into our consciousness.

How could I not like these stories? Like Vicki, I too prefer brevity in discussing What Is. The linear mind, after all, can never grok non-linear Truth. Pointers are given, but the IS remains forever beyond the grasp of our human mind. Now, as ever, our True Self is something that must be remembered, re-seen, re-discovered. Vicki's pieces are like invisible bookmarks, drawing our attention back to the "face we had before we were born."

Always I have been impressed with Vicki's extraordinary willingness to look deep within the eye of human suffering. As most of us know, there is no other way to transcend suffering but to enter into it with an open mind and heart. Is that an easy task? Of course not. It is precisely because it is arduous that we need a Vicki to stand near us while we walk through our prisons of fear and grief and loss—and then, finally, into the silent arms of Freedom. As Jung said, "Enlightenment is not about imagining figures of light, but of making the darkness conscious."

This book is a treasure house of one woman's honest and rigorous journey through loss to Oneness. If you, too, are moving towards Now, towards Here, towards Presence—take Vicki's book with you.

Elsa Joy Bailey,
Concord, CA

We Are Drawn In Disappearing Ink

We are drawn in disappearing ink. Not much use in
wondering why or when we will run dry,
just fade away.

Our minds are drawn; our mouths are pursed.
We know it's all been pre-rehearsed.

Come here, dear character so drawn
and look, there is another dawn.

See, it's way out there beyond your
loves and hates...it rises like a rich red
curtain on the higher world.

—Vicki Woodyard

PROLOGUE

Through Eyes of Wholeness

As I wrote this book, I felt as if my personal heart was being ripped out. I drove myself through the valley of the shadow like a demented shepherdess. I knew no peace and yet I wrote doggedly and exhaustedly. I would not have wanted Vicki to be my caregiver. She was someone in process.

Looking back, I see that the personal trauma was in order to be healed by the universal heart. No one chooses that road or thinks they will survive. Death is inevitable on every level. But so is rebirth. Fortunately I walked in the company of the spirit. I do believe the plan for discovering our inherent wholeness cannot be sabotaged by the ego. The eye of illusion cannot see.

Today the self that I used to be would scarcely be recognized by the one I have become. The eye of wholeness doesn't cry. If you are walking through dark times and feel alone, know that many have gone before you. It is holy ground all the way home.

INTRODUCTION
I Left It All At The Nonduality Salon

These essays, for the most part, made their debut on Jerry Katz's Nonduality Salon. I began my website, *Nurturing the Now*, when my late husband was diagnosed with cancer. I wanted to support him, but as the days went by, I realized I was developing a voice that I needed to share. I began to contribute essays on a regular basis. He was and is a good friend and encourager to many. Thanks, Jerry.

My life was breaking down, but my writing was flowering. Many nights would find me at the computer busily typing the truth of life, converting it into essays and hitting the send button. I was working as hard as I ever worked in my life, being a caregiver and preparing for my husband's death. But the writer in me was flourishing. The phoenix of my passion was rising from the ashes.

I write in order to move you on some primal level. I don't care much if I make you laugh or cry; I just want you to have an experience.

I need to say a few words about my spiritual background. My chief inspiration was Vernon Howard, who lived and taught in Boulder City, Nevada. But the words of Ramana Maharshi, Nisargadatta, and other awakened souls continue to inspire me. Ultimately we are here to learn that we ourselves are the Way.

I was born to the path and will die on it. But in many ways, as I say in the essay, *Enlightenment Is A Dirty Word*, I am not so interested in my own enlightenment. I still have to chop wood and carry water. I hope the essays will bear witness to the truth as I have experienced it.

The title, *Life With A Hole In It*, chose me, as puppies or kittens often do. I had been considering dozens, and none of them really excited me. Then this title suddenly rushed over to me and jumped into my lap and licked the tears off my face. Needless to say, I took it with me and now it has a permanent place in my heart.

I have written about my personal losses, but everyone has a hole in their life of some sort and yet in our core we are always whole. To live with that paradox is to live in peace.

Ground Down

"From the curse comes a blessing.
From nothing comes something."
(Bernie Siegel, MD)

My emotional hands were dirty and callused from living life as
a caregiver for almost five years. It was hot and I spent many an
hour on my knees planting seeds of hope and courage. Not
many sprouted. I looked to heaven and there seemed to come a
great drought of answered prayers.

My husband's health deteriorated as I planted words deep into
the soil of my website. I sweated blood as he continued to walk
toward the other side. He had a death sentence on him and I was
planting seeds as fast as I could. I was desperate.

Although I was born to the spiritual path, I was now spending
time in the dirt, the deep brown stuff from which we all spring.
I was learning to walk the walk. And I wore gardening gloves
and a brimmed hat so no one would see the tears in my eyes. I
was a persistent gardener. Nothing else would do.

A higher force than myself planted the seeds of my writing, or
so it seemed to me. I was following orders instinctively to keep
planting the words. Every now and again someone would write
and say the words they read were feeding them. And a silent
hallelujah would rise up within me.

My husband died, but the planting never stopped. As I continue
to write, there is a continual blooming into awareness and a
return to the place I never left.

Just Beyond Splat

A disciple hit the wall one day and asked his guru where all of his good feelings had gone. "Just beyond splat," the guru said, "just beyond splat."

And so it goes. Right now snow is hitting the roof like hard rain because it IS hard rain. The weatherman missed his forecast of snow. Life is like that. It is also like Forrest Gump's box of chocolates. You never know what you are going to get. Rain is wrapped up in a forecast of snow, love is wrapped up in death and time is what you never have enough of when someone you love is dying.

Nevertheless I travel on through snow and sleet and splat. I offer you this collection of words as leftovers from my banquet of life. Nuke them until your heart is warm and then throw the container in the trash. Waste nothing. Use everything. If snow is pelting your roof, just know that somewhere, people are shoveling rain, not expecting it to come in that form.

I love words but only when I can use them as something else— as a key to the heart.

The Ultimate Intimacy

Knowing yourself as the Self is the ultimate intimacy. Unconditional love for yourself arises. You don't do anything but sit in the silence, inviting peace. I usually say, "I am in God's presence now," and relax into the silence that is always immediately there.

It took me a long time to get to this place. I studied truth for years and years and then one day I had effortless access, sort of like an ATM machine with no limits. I have had no enlightenment experience, rather, one crisis after another over a period of many years.

Lately I have been reading many accounts of people who have awakened and I know that I am not there yet.

"Are we there yet, are we there yet?" ask the spiritual seeking children in the backseat of the enlightenment limo. Those who have arrived have a lot to say about the silence. Much of it is helpful and most is not.

The most helpful information comes from those who do not wax overly eloquent. Although I have read tons of tomes, usually they did not have the energy contained in some of the pithier statements. I guess it's like the guy said, "If I had had more time, I could have written you a shorter letter."

Find an energy statement that works for you and work it. Here are a few of my favorites:

Let it have you.

Let everything unfold.

I choose to love myself.

And finally, meditate on the word *inevitability.*

We will get there when we get there—inevitably.

Enlightenment Is A Dirty Word

Enlightenment has become almost a dirty word with me. I have strived for it, studied for it, let go of it, clung to it, danced with it, and tranced with it. I have gone the extra mile for it, flashed the smile for it, hoping that someday, somehow, it would be given to me as an act of grace.

I should know better. I studied with a master teacher, Vernon Howard. There was no question about his enlightenment. Every word he said was true and came from the depths of the inner heights. His energy was phenomenal, pure and transcendent. I wanted a piece of it.

He died of cancer. His secretary befriended me and she died of cancer. Now my husband has incurable cancer. Somewhere along the line I have become less excited about my own particular nirvana.

During the worst days, my husband was so ill he did not know where he was. I knew all too well where I was—in hell. One day when he was in the hospital I came home and sat down at the computer. All of a sudden my bowels released and I messed in the computer chair. I cleaned myself up. The dog had thrown up on my side of the bed near my pillow. I stepped in dog doody and walked it all over the hospital corridors. And strangely enough I knew that I was getting a message of love— of the Mother Teresa variety. I was the unclean person.

I also knew during this strange time of trial that every time I asked for something I would be given an inner message that things would go better if I let things come to me unasked. I was in a No Man's Land. Who cared about enlightenment when there were unmentionable sufferings occurring in my life? Who cared?

My husband's ribs had been broken by the undiagnosed cancer and he looked like a skeleton. Since our daughter had died of the disease as a child, I knew what death looked like. I didn't want it to happen to him. When he got home from the hospital I slept with a skeleton for months.

Now he is in remission but I have much more self-esteem than I did when I was seeking enlightenment. Enlightenment is cellular—unearned and undiscerned. It is ephemeral, visceral and gut-wrenching.

People tell me that I have an aura of peace about me. I know what they mean, for when I look inside I experience it. The sad thing is that my ego with the name and form must undergo panic attacks and frequent sorrow because she can never be enlightened.

I am tired of reading all the endless names of people who teach enlightenment. They have books and tapes and seminars and retreats and introductory trial offers. I know the same things that they do—more's the pity.

If you would like to consult with me about gut-wrenching loneliness contained within a peaceful energy field, be my guest. I just don't do seminars.

Barely There

I am barely there. I don't mean that I am almost not here. I mean that I am here in a very bare way. Nude in the way that it counts—in a psychological way. I am a Scorpio through and through and I calls 'em like I sees 'em.

This lends itself to writing one-liners, both comedic and spiritual. I like to hit people hard with what I have come to say. Maybe that is because I have been hit so hard and for so long.

It was cancer that wreaked havoc on my life. No, I have never had it myself. I would have preferred it that way. The hand that I have been dealt is that of a hand-holder. I have also held more than my fair share of emesis basins, both pink plastic and cold stainless steel. The old "urp pan," as we used to call it.

My daughter died of cancer when she was seven years old. She was barely here before she left. Undoubtedly, she came to earth with a mission to sow love and succeeded mightily; but the way in which she died shouldn't happen to anyone.

We kept her at home until the last five days. When, she ran out of oxygen except in the tip of one lung, we were advised that if we wanted her to die in the hospital, it was time. Her life was brief and to the point. She laughed, she loved and she left us all with a giant question, but we didn't even know what it was. It was more like an ache that we wanted answered.

I had cranked out one-liners for standup comedians for quite a while. It kept me busy while I was raising my daughter and her older brother. I was hilarious while driving my Smith-Corona typewriter, but the mileage was miserable. The pay was even worse. The lowest pay I ever got was from Phyllis Diller. She bought a joke for one dollar, calling it B grade and then she used it on the Tonight Show. Go figure.

There Is An Opening

There is an opening that you must step through. It is called lowliness. Raynor C. Johnson, author of *The Spiritual Path,* said that *the spiritual path is like walking through an archway of humility, where the keys of love and trust will open every door that bars your way.* We do not hear that kind of talk these days. We call it old-fashioned or needlessly simple. Nevertheless, it is a most valuable admonition.

Lowliness is thrust upon us in some situations. Often the dark night of the soul is a precursor to this state. For example, when my husband was first diagnosed with cancer and was in the hospital for weeks, I also had to contend with having lowliness thrust in my face, like the day I tracked dog doody all over the hospital corridors. In some uncanny bit of self-insight I knew that it was the holiest time for me. I accepted all of it as being part of the divine design.

Later there would be horrific pieces of my lowliness that I had to see and incorporate into my life. Prideful crowing about how well I was dealing with his illness was not on the agenda. Instead I found myself sputtering, cursing and soaking the pillowcase with tears. I went to the drugstore to buy an alarm clock with a luminous dial so that when I shot bolt upright in bed over and over, I could see what time it was. I had to push a button to get the clock to light up, so I slept with it beside me in bed. The numbers were jumbo-sized and I could see that indeed it was 2:30, then 3:30, etc.

I was not prepared for being a caregiver. It was wrenched out of me, dreadful bit by dreadful bit. There were no holy choirs hovering over me as I slept—just a stupid plastic clock with king-sized numbers. And there were other things. I found that I had no desire to talk on the phone. When I did, I ranted on and on about my suffering. I didn't care that I was driving people away. I was speaking my truth.

It was only when I begin writing that I found solace. My computer willingly recorded every emotion that I typed in. It offered me blank space in my personal world gone mad. Lowliness was beginning to be replaced by certain principles of organization. I learned that I liked being organized. That if my place was to be lowly it could still be neat. I began outfitting the house in a practical way and soon I began feeling more like my old self.

Something called complacency had been sandblasted away in that terrible shock of an incurable diagnosis. God knew what He was doing after all. Now all I needed to do was trust Him.

Several years have passed in this way, not doing anything but coping with caregiving and writing as I can find time. I am no less sorrowful about my husband's diagnosis but I have incorporated it into my life. It is a life that belongs fully to me. If I grieve, it is my grief. Growth is a concentric thing and following the labyrinth of my life is a good thing for me to do.

Living a spiritual life requires a lot of admitting that one is not living a spiritual life. Peter Matthiessen, in *Nine-Headed Dragon River*, says this of Dogen, *Having met with his own Buddha-nature, Dogen seems to have become less judgmental, less demanding. Asked what he had learned abroad, he said, "Not much except a tender spirit."*

The tender spirit can only be a witness to what is not tender, is yet insensitive and hypocritical. When I catch myself wondering what these ancient Zen masters have to do with me, I am just being tough on myself once again. Buddha-nature knows this.

"In my visits to my teacher I noticed
a change many years ago.
Her house has always been silent.
Now the silence began to rip every illusion apart."
(Alan Larus)

Priceless

We have all watched the MasterCard commercial where certain experiences are called "priceless." But we ourselves are priceless.

You, in your essence, are the pearl of great price, the Beloved. Yes, you. When was the last time, if ever, you looked at the truth of your being and rejoiced? Probably never. Most of us look on ourselves with jaundiced weary eyes, while we look at bonded teeth and hair weaves with envy and a sense that we will never look perfect.

I remember when my young daughter was dying. She lost all of her hair to chemo at age four. Pale as a ghost and with a scar that ran down her right thigh, she did the hula for us on her unscathed leg. She had a malignant tumor in the muscle of her right one. So as she got her chemo at St. Jude Children's Research Hospital and her father returned to work, we told her to surprise him with the hula. That six-foot four-inch man turned to mush, of course. She knew she was dying; don't ask me how. We tried to keep it from her, but she looked at my brother one fine day and said, "You know, don't you?"

Yes, we were all in on the conspiracy. The priceless one in her would never die, though. She would be in her thirties now and she is one reason I still write. To celebrate the truth of our being.

In 2000, I became a caregiver for the second time in my life when Bob was diagnosed. I railed against circumstance for the four years that he fought the disease. One of the hardest things I ever had to hear came from a hospital chaplain. "Your husband

14

is staying alive to take care of you," he told me solemnly as I sat in his office. After hearing that, I went back to my husband's hospital room and told him I would be all right without him.

When he died, I discovered that his essence remains, in all of its priceless wonder. When I took a vacation this spring, after many years of staying at home, he came to me in a dream the week after I got back. I felt an electronic buzz in my body as he hugged me. He spoke no words—just let me know he was glad I was moving on.

You probably have your own memories of someone who has gone on. Let it be that way. Fighting it will never resolve your own knowing. And that knowing itself is priceless. The real can never be taken from us. The unreal never was ours to begin with.

Celebrate yourself any time you can. Do this by entering the silence in quiet recognition that love, which you are, can never die. Choose life in the right sense. Choose to love yourself and then you love the universe as well. If you choose to love the universe first, you will be leaving yourself out. This is a conundrum that thought can never solve. Let something higher show you how powerful loving yourself can be.

The Psychotic Break

Bob had been losing weight and color for months. His doctor misdiagnosed him as having bowel problems and set him up to have tests done with a gastroenterologist. Before that happened, he got so ill my son and I took him to the Emergency Room. "Your husband," said the admitting doctor, "is a very sick man. He has calcium in his blood stream. It's a wonder he is not hallucinating." (That would come later.)

He was admitted to the hospital and the barrage of tests began. I heard the diagnosis indirectly. I was talking to Bob on the phone and an oncologist came into his room. I heard him say, "I'll let you know when we can begin chemo."

I gasped. Bob had been crying. The doctor had just diagnosed him with multiple myeloma. His father had died of it at age sixty-three. A port was installed in his chest on a Thursday morning and the chemo began that very night. As the nurse hung the bottles of chemo, she said casually, "Let me know if you have any side effects; sometimes these meds can give you some strange results."

All of his physicians were unavailable until Monday morning. By Saturday he was hallucinating. He gained twelve pounds overnight from steroids in his IV. He was like a crazy person, making notes in a binder that went on and on and on. He was clearly on a "trip" of some sort.

By mid-week he had no idea where he was. I was home resting when the head nurse called. "Your husband," she said, "broke all the IV lines and de-accessed his port. We caught him as he was roaming the halls. You better get down here."

By the time I arrived and walked in his room, this is what I found—a man sitting on his bed fully dressed and beaming with joy to see me. "I was coming home to you—to see you, Angel," he said. "I got dressed and was coming home."

He had been given an enema (multiple myeloma causes severe constipation) and had messed in his pants. I gagged. He was blissfully unaware. His pants pockets were full of the change I had left him for cokes and snacks. My heart was full of despair.

The nurse said, "Mr. Woodyard was sticking manicure scissors into the electrical outlet. He had packed up everything in the room and was going to walk home. But he's better now, aren't you?" she said, looking into his face.

The next three weeks were spent in the hospital with a crazy man. He was put on the proper drugs for the psychosis induced by the steroids. I had to go through it my own way. One night I was in the family lounge and a group of people were in there. I blurted out the whole sad story and one of the wives could relate. "My husband, "she said, "had a bad reaction to the steroids as well."

"Yes," he said, "I was watching movies on the window in my room and trying to get someone, anyone, to put mustard on the giant hot dog at the foot of my bed."

I had tracked in dog doody on my shoe that morning and had come in the lounge restroom to wash it off. I found myself crying and laughing as I told what had happened to Bob.

The next bad news also came to me indirectly. I could not bring myself to go to the oncologist with Bob for his first visit after he got home from the hospital, so our son went with him. They took a tape recorder. A few weeks later I decided I would play it to hear what the doctor had said. It said, in so many words, "You have less than three years."

Why Not Golden Light?

After Bob's reaction to his powerful chemo, his personality altered dramatically until slowly he got the drugs out of his system. They put him on a close watch. A couple of nights into it, I got a call. "Mrs. Woodyard, you need to get down here." It was the night nurse.

"Your husband has been singing and not wanting to sleep. He seems very agitated." Her voice had a lovely Caribbean lilt to it. "I just sang along with him," she said. "I think he'll be all right, but you might want to come and be with him."

So another exhausting round began. Bob was in love with life on this chemical high. After I got home that night for a few hours of rest, our son stayed with him. He called the next morning to let me know about a night-long lovefest. "Dad stood up all night and made me hold hands with him," he said. "He was hooked up to his IV and the two of us stood there—with him saying 'I love you' to me over and over and over."

When I arrived at the hospital, I, too, was bathed in his love. Every now and again, he would need to use the bathroom. He made me stand right outside the door, saying "Are you there? I love you. Are you there?"

I bought him a small brown dog from the cheer cart. He couldn't believe that I had done such a thing for him. His eyes told the story. He was in love with a great force. Life and love and death and suffering had mingled into one big smorgasbord of love for Bob. He was imbibing light.

The downside of this was paranoia. He made me bring water from home. This was, he said, to prevent the hospital from poisoning him. "Come here, I want to tell you something," he said from his bed.

I leaned down close to him and he said, "The man who shaves me—he wants to take me out of here in a box." I listened, patting his hand.

"He wants to get rid of me."

"Oh, no, he's a very nice man," I said, seeing the folly of arguing with someone who was delusional.

"No, no. He wants me dead."

He didn't want visitors, but every now and then someone snuck in. A man he barely knew ignored the No Visitors sign because he was a "good friend." Later, Bob told me that he saw bad energy leave this man's stomach area and try to enter his body. For some reason, I believed him. Heightened sensitivity is sometimes right on the money. He also received an expensive flower arrangement from a man he had worked with. "Take them out of here," Bob told me. "They have bad energy in them." And I did.

One afternoon Bob looked into my eyes and said, "I saw the mountain top and the golden light. I want you to take me there." I told him I would. I was already bringing him drinking water— why not golden light?

There Is Only Everything

Most of us on the spiritual path have been on it for longer than we care to admit. At least that is the case with me. Suffering, sorrow and struggle have taken their toll. I am now willing to admit something—there is only everything.

Apparently I wasn't wise enough to come to this conclusion any earlier. Like Irina Tweedie, who wrote *Daughter of Fire*, my inner sheik has been holding my feelings to the fire for far too long. But I'm now willing to admit it. There is only everything.

In spite of having mystical dreams and synchronistic situations, it just wasn't enough for me. I wanted cosmic visions and the rarity of sat-chit-ananda. It wasn't to be.

Instead I got "I-opening" sorrow, self-searing introspection and many dark nights of the soul. Some got so dark I bumped into the universal furniture until my shins were blue.

But just lately, I am opening up to a wider wisdom—there is only everything. And it seems that everything is enough. The Popsicle Man comes along the street with his truckful of colorful flavors and we think we must make a decision. Do I want lime or grape or cherry enlightenment? The mind must have its favorite flavor. So we let it do its thing. My advice— pay the Popsicle Man and get on with your life.

My life is currently breaking down and I see that this is freeing. Like a little child, all the flavors of life have stained my white shirt and there is little chance that I can get the stains out on my own for there is no "my own." There is only everything.

It didn't have to be so hard. I could have had my flavor of the day and every other flavor to boot. My choices were not mine anyway. They belonged to the mind, which is now falling away as fast as I can allow it.

The wisdom of life is inherent in unity and only in unity. But we can only arrive there when we understand that there never had to be a problem in deciding what flavor of life we wanted that day. Everything comes in an astonishing variety and everything is all there really is.

Buddha's Secret

The Buddha is a shadowy figure at best to me. Try as I might, I can never remember what it was that he said exactly. Frankly, I just remember how he looks. Fat little guy with bare feet and his hands thrown upwards into the air. Quite possibly he was an early weatherman, who knows.

Of course, sometimes he is seated in a reflective posture. He is more than likely counting his fat rolls, love handles, mayonnaise—call it what you will. Let's be frank; the Buddha was obese. If he had to have his body fat ratio calculated, it would not have been a pretty picture.

Didn't he say that all of life is suffering? I know that I have been suffering ever since I sat down at the computer to write this piece.

Buddha is a buddy of mine. I met him at the Waffle House and he bought me a cup of joe and sat with me in Buddha posture as he buttered his waffle. He seemed unattached to the outcome of eating all of those waffles.

"Buddha, buddy," I asked him, "aren't you worried about your cholesterol count? Are you on Zocor or Lipitor yet?"

He regarded me quizzically and said nothing. He chewed and swallowed each morsel daintily. His aura was redolent of bacon grease.

As he got up to leave, I cautioned him that he shouldn't travel alone, as people might try to kill him if they met him on the road. "Not to worry," said the round little man, "if my disciples don't kill me, the waffles will."

"Then why don't you quit eating waffles and for heaven's sake, stop being a Buddha. Just be ordinary. Then no one would try to kill you."

"You don't understand," he said wearily. "I am ordinary. That is what makes me the Buddha. It's you disciples who are trying to make me extraordinary. If you knew how ordinary I was, you would let me eat my waffles in peace. You would let me go and come to your senses."

I opened the door of the Waffle House and let him precede me into the cold, dark night. His secret is safe with me.

I Don't Aspire To Buddhahood — It Would Just Make Me Look Fat

I gave up seeking enlightenment when I realized that Buddhahood would just make me look fat.

We are told to kill the Buddha if we meet him on the road. Judging from his depictions in art down through the ages, we are more apt to meet him at The Waffle House. I bet the Buddha liked buttah.

But kill him at The Waffle House? C'mon. I couldn't kill anybody at the Waffle House, especially Buddha.

If Buddha and I occupied a booth at the Waffle House, we would probably say nothing except "pass the syrup," and that surreptitiously. Nothing of an enlightening nature would be transmitted. His secret is safe with me.

I might secretly long for him to give me the transmission, and maybe even an extra set of windshield wipers, but I would never press him.

Frankly, the Buddha is trying to get away from people. After all, people don't want enlightenment. They want a Buddha pat. They want the Buddha to tell them that they don't have to change. Don't you think he's getting a little tired of that? He knows that there is no one there to change. (by the way, I hope they don't have one of those No Shirt, No Shoes, No Service signs because the Buddha is barefoot.) I find myself trying to divert the waitress's attention from this fact, but she is looking at the Buddha boobs, pretty impressive for a man.

"Honey," she says to Buddha Man, "Can I get you some more coffee?"

Buddha just looks at her and winks. Wait a minute—could this be Santa just out of the sauna?

Whoever....

If you meet Buddha and me at the Waffle House, don't kill us. We'll just get a bigger booth and you can join us.

Into The Darkness

I am tired of hearing so much about the bliss and peace of being in the light. Most of us wouldn't recognize true peace if it came up to us in the mall and introduced itself. We are too busy scouring the sales racks and scowling at our faces in the mirrored windows of all the stores. Enough is enough already.

True spirituality requires a downward turn into the darkness of your own private hell. Of course it is so covered over in materiality that it is hard to find the entrance. But you don't have to look very far. The next twinge of inner pain is being brought to you courtesy of the darkness. Go toward the darkness now!

I avoid my own darkness like the plague. That is precisely why it is still there. The parts of it that I have had the courage to examine have strangely evaporated. I wonder why. Could it be...no...yes...it's because consciousness is stronger than darkness and we are consciousness itself.

Somehow or another we have been sold a bill of goods by so many peddlers of the positive path. This path exists all right, but it is bought with a price. It is not the free and easy satori that you think it is. It is just the opposite. When I catch myself getting too saccharine it is because I am buying into the false notion that I can be either good or bad. In reality, I am just pure consciousness.

Going into the darkness means that you are ready to face the truth about yourself. To speak personally, my own darkness seems to follow me like my shadow. And I am still afraid of it.

Intellectually, I know that it is just one part of myself running from another part, but I get snookered by it all day long. I might be smart enough to guess which pea is under which shell in the old con game, but I seem to have trouble distinguishing between one me and another me. Odd, isn't it? Once we find the courage to enter the darkness, it dissipates. This is how I know that God exists. He is walking with me through the valley of the shadow of my mind.

Laughter seems to help. If you can't take time out for a good honest laugh at the whole mess, maybe you are a candidate for pure positive thinking. Not me. I'm headed for the biggest patch of darkness that I can find. Once I have entered a new patch of inner pain and stayed with it, I am certain to find the light. That's the formula, folks. Beam me down, Scottie.

Starting Life All Over

I was sitting in my chair this morning with thoughts of the last several days running through my mind. Tuesday my husband received a massive dose of chemotherapy and the next forty-eight hours passed in a slow motion of agony for both of us. On Wednesday night a raccoon chewed a hole in our chimney and set up housekeeping. I hated him with all of my pent-up emotions. Last night our old dog's legs just gave out as we came in the house after she did her business. I sat next to her on the floor and wept like a baby. I talked to her and she wagged her tail and gazed at me from blind eyes. I carried her to her bed and finally, another long day had come to an end.

This morning the sun is out and the cherry tree in our front yard is in bloom. The bees are buzzing around the phlox and someone is here to replace some boards on the house. I took a walk and was aware of blue sky, tall trees and spring. The war in Iraq has receded in my mind as my husband fights to get his cancer back in remission. Such is the personal awareness.

As I continue to sit in my chair and experience peace, I am reminded that wholeness is the goal for all of us. The compartmentalized mind will never secure peace. Even though suffering abounds, so does its remedy, which is being whole. It takes no effort to be whole, just intention.

My intention is to be what I need to have, to rise above the opposites and live in paradox. I never succeed at this because the world will continue to make its demands on me, yet my goal is assured. At some precious moment I will let go and start life all over. I wish the same for you.

One Day Is The Last Day

Christy was almost seventeen and had become blind, deaf and severely confused. We brought her home as a six-week-old Bichon Frise puppy. She had an innate sense of comic timing, better than Berle, born for the Borscht circuit. "Take my leash, please." She kept us on our toes.

We trod through grass, slogged through mud, and brought it all indoors on our floors, making dirt a nondual experience for us. We watched as she managed to pull up a section of old carpet with her teeth. She teethed on the stone fireplace and once chewed off every single pearl button on one of my prettiest gowns.

As she grew older and blinder, we began to have to carry her in and out to do her business. Heck, much of the time she just did it on the floor. We walked around the house much like Python people from the Ministry of Silly Walks. We all knew that her days were numbered.

She never got too old to enjoy begging for chicken and turkey when we ate lunch. When my son told his Japanese girlfriend that Christy had died, she was shocked. "I always remember her standing on a chair saying, "Give me chicken!"

We bought her a rainbow-colored sweater this winter after the groomer cut off all of her beautiful coat because she got too tired to endure the grooming process. In what must have been a "Miracle at Canine" when we were out of the room, her paws turned into hands—and the silly sweater was found lying on the floor as Christy walked casually into the kitchen bare once again.

Monday morning we knew that it was time to put Christy down. She had stopped eating her dog food and was only skin and bones. She managed to eat chicken twice that day, though. Tears slipped down my face as I fed her. My son and I took her to the vets and left her there in their loving care. "Am I doing the right thing?" I asked.

"There is no doubt in my mind," he said. I offered Christy to him. "This is a labor of love for me," he said gently and said that he would put her down as soon as we left.

One day is the last day. She won't be there in her little Bichon body any longer and grief for a family pet is real. My spiritual teacher's secretary told me once that I was a slave to a dog and she was right. I am not ready to take on such attachment again. But I think that my code word for I deserve to be happy is gonna be, "Give me chicken!"

Satsang With Elvis

Going down into the depths is healing, no matter how hard it may seem. Normally, we descend mechanically, causing ourselves to fall under the spell of negativity and gloom. Once we choose a conscious descent, everything is instantly transmuted into light. The truth becomes as clear as aqua waters—we are everything. No more dividing, depressing and destroying. We can begin to unite, uplift and recreate.

I was born in Memphis, Tennessee and watched Elvis rise to fame. He was a polite young man who never forgot where he came from. I was watching a program on PBS about him tonight. "He Touched Me" is full of hymns that make me cry. Before I know it, the depths have overwhelmed me and the tears are flowing. I have to stop, blow my nose and remember that I am the Self in all beings. It is that simple and that difficult. It must be done. It is the basis of all spiritual work.

Simplicity is such a healing agent. We are moved by Elvis Presley's devotion to the old gospel tunes. We must stand by the Self that we are, descending into our spiritual roots. And oh, it is hard to do. The little grave where my daughter lies buried is in Memphis, too. The last time I visited it, the sun was shining and we were at peace with her death. How incredible that we have survived this long without her. I often feel like an empty shell. I write and write about simple spirituality and how we must face our suffering. I never want to do it. Never.

I also say how tired I get of sophisticated nondualism; the kind that turns you into a snob. It is easy to sit in satsang with people who have never really suffered. But those of us who have must tell it like it is. My friend Peter says he gave up on satsang long ago and now has it with his cat, Alex. I understand where he is coming from. He says that in spite of himself he has become bigger than the sky. When he writes me, it is to remind me of the sweetness of the living moment. When the tears slip down my cheeks, I must wake up, allow them to be there and know that there is only the Self. It is a must-have realization.

Weakness Is Not The Problem

My weakness is not the problem; I only think it is. The real problem is my lack of surrender. Anything given to God is tended like a garden. Turned over like the good earth. Made more fruitful than before. I keep forgetting the most basic facts about myself. My strength is rendered weakness when I turn away from God and try to depend upon myself.

My fragility is not an issue; I only think it is. The basic issue is my lack of trust in God. He can mend the broken hearts surrendered to His care. I always forget.

My feeling of being unloved and unlovable is never true. Only God is true and He says that He cares for me like a sparrow. Like a dove with a broken wing. I just don't get the simplest things about how God works.

Is it because I want Him to operate like an ATM machine? Of course. Is it because He doesn't heal the sick when I demand that He do? Obviously.

That is why I am mad at God. He doesn't always heal the sick. He doesn't always let the blind see or the lame walk. Damn it.

My anger is not the problem; I only think it is. The real problem is my human grief. Who but God gave me the eyes to cry? Who but Him can stop the tears? No one.

I forget.

Riding The Horse Of Fear

Dr. Bernie Siegel uses the expression *ride the horse of fear* when he is talking to cancer patients. This is a man who has revolutionized the way that we look at cancer. He has given patients the urge and the methods to turn their challenges into changes for the better.

We all keep horses of fear in our subconscious stables. We feed them and shelter them, so of course they breed. What if we did as Bernie said and rode our horses of fear consciously? After all, they are there in our unconscious minds. We are giving them shelter; we might as well ride them.

To give you an example from my own life, I have always had a fear of being a strong personality. My father was a troubled man, prone to angry outbursts and fits of pique. As a child, I learned to be compliant and overly accommodating, first to my father and later to the entire world. Quite a job and I did it well. When I began having panic attacks and agoraphobia when I was in my early teens, I squelched the terror and never spoke of it. I was riding the horse of fear unconsciously and mechanically.

As an adult, I still have an unrealistic fear of social condemnation. That is probably why I wrote one-liners for standup comedians for many years. I could put my words in their mouths. I could get a modest check and vent my spleen at the same time. But this didn't help my fear of what other people thought of me.

Then I began walking the spiritual path and it is largely about overcoming fear and all of the other negative emotions. I had so many horses in the barn that I didn't know which one I would be riding on any given day. Fear, shame, and guilt were all in the stables of my soul.

When my husband was diagnosed, the horse of fear that the disease created was so huge that I thought I would never have the courage to even get upon its back. Its nostrils flared; its mane was a deep dark black. I paled at the prospect.

Days in the hospital turned into weeks and every day I had to get up on that horse and ride to the hospital. Tears blinded my eyes as I rode, but the horse would not veer from carrying me into the pain and the sorrow that someone feels when their loved one is diagnosed with cancer.

On the day that he was diagnosed, I walked down the corridors of the hospital and into my husband's room. He had been taken down for x-rays and there was only a nurse named Gertie in there. I wept. "Gertie, close the door," I said. "You have to help me. I have got to get myself together."

Gertie was a very spiritual person; I had sensed that immediately when she was first assigned to care for my husband. She had, in fact, administered his first chemotherapy. She was a warrior soul.

Gertie and I prayed together. I have no idea what words were said. I remember telling her that I would make it through this somehow—that God would guide me. It was by telling Gertie what I believed that I first began riding the horse of fear consciously. Before, I had let the horse take me down the path with no clear awareness. I was resisting its direction. Now it hit me like a thunderbolt. I would no longer resist riding it. I would be in charge. God would not let me fail. Gertie and I gathered so much good energy that we could have lifted the ceiling off of that hospital room. My sorrow had taken a new direction.

Over two years have gone by since my husband was diagnosed. Even though he is out of remission and beginning more chemo, I am still willing to ride the horse of fear. But instead of the horse coming for me, I often choose to go to the stables and let the horse know that I will be in charge of the ride that day.

Choosing to ride the horse of fear can change your life instantly. You can turn on a dime. God's gift of courage comes to those who want to wake up and handle the challenges of life as He would have us do. It doesn't matter how many times you fall off, either. Sometimes the horse throws me into mud puddles and this is when I doubt if I am doing the right thing. I appear to be losing the battle with fear. I begin to doubt myself.

Fear is a part of the human condition—yours, mine and everyone else's. But here is the challenge and the solution rolled into one. Ride the horse of fear consciously. Choose it. Resistance to fear is what perpetuates it. We all know this. It doesn't matter whether your challenge is cancer or not, ride the horse of fear by your own choice.

My husband's cancer has opened up inner depths in me that I did not know I had. Some were good and others bad, yet they both needed to be looked at. Our humanity is heightened as we honor our fears and go with them in a new direction. Perhaps your horse of fear wants to take you into the dark night of your soul just so you can get it over with. At the end of the journey is a blinding light of belief. You begin to believe in yourself.

Fear never goes away entirely because of the fact that we are human. Even Christ suffered when He was tested. I will bet that the horses of fear in your stable are anxious for you to take them for a ride. But do it consciously. Remember the advice of Bernie Siegel and ride the horse of fear. And let me know how it works out for you.

Surrender Is The Only Safe Place

Those who are undergoing sorrow and suffering feel totally alone. Often this is referred to as the dark night of the soul, especially when you have been on the spiritual path. When all is failing you, or seeming to, you are forced to sit alone and endure the sorrow consciously.

The paradox of pain is that in that dark night, the inner stars come out. These simple stars of sorrow are shining for a reason. There is a beauty in surrender that can now begin to illuminate your "I."

There is safety in surrender—and also spiritual instruction. Surrender teaches us that the only safety we will ever know is in letting things go on exactly as they must. Resistance is mental and emotional and therefore draining. Surrender is spiritual and gives us the energy of peace.

The peace of surrender is energizing. It sets in motion your own unseen healing forces that cannot come into play while you are fighting your situation. Tears are simply allowed, anger is seen but not resisted, futility is witnessed without a fight.

I am speaking from personal experience—from a heart that has been too often broken. Yet only when I sit and surrender do I feel the peace of God arising from within. My little surrendered moments are hugely powerful, as are yours. They are able to energize my entire day. I know and say with certainty that surrender is the most underrated little word there is. Try it.

The Well-Dressed Mind

What is the well-dressed mind wearing these days? Does it wear Eckhart Tolle like a stole? Deepak like Reebok? I want my mind to go to a nude beach and wear its birthday suit. There it could recline on the sand and fan itself with the fronds from a nearby palm.

Nothingness is what the well-dressed mind should be wearing. No Vera Wang, no Tommy Hilfiger, just nothing, bare beingness. You shouldn't even need to wear a sunscreen or an aluminum hat like in the movie *Signs*. No, you gotta have faith in stark reality.

I want my mind to kick off its shoes. No Manolo Blahniks for these tootsies. No Dr. Scholl's for the soul. Nope. I don't need any mental Frederick's of Hollywood either. Twoness is not what it's about, girls. Actually, tell that one to the men.

You gotta have heart to go nude in your own mind. No belief system covering up your private parts. No girdle smothering your innermost thoughts and feelings. Just the facts, ma'am, just the facts. And the fact is, the mind is as unreal as its clothes. Now don't go telling that to your shrink. That would put him out of business. Keep it to yourself.

There is only one problem with the mind's nudity. When it returns to the garden (and I don't mean Madison), it will have to meet the snake. I have been told that the snake is a rope, though this has not been scientifically proven. So when you meet the snake, don't take a bite of the apple and you'll be fine. And if you do, grab a fig leaf and hold on. But that's another story.

Everything I Know About Enlightenment I Learned In Kindergarten

Enlightenment is something that I continue to think about. If understanding is the booby prize, can enlightenment be far behind? Just what the heck is it that I am supposed to do? Lord knows I have striven until I am as blue in the face as Krishna.

Don't get me wrong. I am as determined as the next guy to win the elusive prize because then I could go on the lecture circuit and tell the unwashed unenlightened a thing or two.

I would start with this, a grand summary of all the best axioms. Don't put a head on top of your head. The wind is blowing, not the flag. Put down that woman, you're still carrying her. Hey, dope, that's a snake, not a rope. I am just a finger pointing toward the moon. I am sitting by the river selling river water. And perhaps my favorite, Stop! My cup is overflowing. I have always wanted a bigger cup size. Here, here, a toast of river water to the unwashed unenlightened.

Okay, okay, I get it. I already have it. It must be contagious. But there's no cure for the enlightenment bug. It is going to drive you to think—to think about how nice it would feel to be enlightened. Our birthright has been snatched from us, recycled and sold to us as Enlightenment Puffs.

And mantras. Don't get me started. We use mantras all day long. "I don't need this, I don't want this, I can't stand that." Or "Here, give it to me, I need it, where can I get this wholesale?"

Joko Beck tells a story about a man who was waiting for the enlightenment train. While he was waiting he busied himself

41

taking care of others who were waiting and so he forgot that he was waiting—until he no longer cared about his own enlightenment.

You see, it's not that we choose to do good deeds while awaiting our ultimate enlightenment. It's the way that God has set up this paradoxical thing called life. It is how things work. If you really want to be enlightened, you must wait your turn. Be polite, don't push, respect your elders, etc.

The people inside the enlightenment seminars are being told the same things that their mothers and fathers told them. It's just couched in different terms. *Namaste* just means be nice to people, *satsang* is birds of a feather flocking together, and seeing God in everyone is Aretha singing *R-e-s-p-e-c-t.*

A Mind Full Of Light

"A drop of water has the tastes of the water of the seven seas:
there is no need to experience all the ways of worldly life. The
reflections of the moon on one thousand rivers are from the
same moon: the mind must be full of light."
(Hung Tzu-ch'eng, 1593-1665)

How do you get a mind full of light? That is an intriguing
question. Like a dipper of cold water, a mind full of light would
be soothing to the parched soul. Enlightenment must equal that.

But wait a minute. Hang on a sec; there is no mind. It has been
said, however, that when the mind is still it can reflect the Self.
That is why we sit in meditation, pray, do zazen, whirl, and so
forth. We want what we haven't got, a mind full of light.

I am not such a good student of Zen koans. To me the sound of
one hand clapping is pretty clear. A dog has Buddha-nature and
you can't put a head on top of a head, but I am getting off topic.
I see that someone has put up a sign saying, "Mind has just been
mopped. Stay off of it." Okay, okay.

Right now I am in the school cafeteria of life and as usual I
have put more on my tray than I can eat. First I grabbed
dessert—lemon icebox pie. Then I saw clear red cubes of Jell-o
and grabbed that too. Next came fried chicken and mashed
potatoes and green beans—gotta have a yeast roll and a cup of
coffee. That'll be—how much?!

I sat down with some other students and saw that they had done
the same thing. Bitten off more than they could chew. Karma,
predestination, free will, nonduality all look pretty tasty until

you start to consume your attachments. Belly ache, get the Pepto, call the witch doctor—where's a good shaman when you need her?

I had completely forgotten that I wanted a mind full of light— an empty tray sitting serenely, reflecting light from the overhead fluorescent bulb. I come to myself—hear dishes banging, silverware clanking and water running. I just sit and take it all in. So that's how I get a mind full of light. Neat.

The Chemo Room

The chemo room was, as usual, filled with extraordinary people. I spoke with a woman who has metastasized breast cancer and goes to The Wellness Community as do we. We spoke of walls and hearts and true friends, schedules dominated by cancer treatments and all that they entail. I told her that I was ready to take down my wall. "You can," she said, "for I have taken down mine." Her eyes were washed with tears of empathy and I hugged her gently, for she is such a treasure.

There was a woman who had just had a port installed in her chest earlier that morning and her husband sat down in the chair across from me. These two were life partners, no doubt about it. She spoke of her azalea garden even as she fished a book on Braves baseball from her purse. Tamara, the chemo nurse, was showing us pictures of her daughter who had just graduated. You see, we are family to each other. No appointment needed to get a hug or wipe a tear. We are there anyway; we might as well be there for each other.

Yesterday I saw a therapist to get some help in dealing with all of this stress and sorrow. He helped me by confirming my path. He is a writer, too, and we talked of the wind horse way and courage and web pages. He stuck an acupuncture needle in my ear and I wore it proudly into the barbecue joint where we ate after my appointment.

But this was the best thing of all. Someone sent me this email:

> Thank you for embracing the good, the bad, and the
> ugly, as well as the beautiful. Your thoughts speak more
> of spirituality to me than religion.
> (from a 69 year old clean and sober AA member)

That letter makes it all worthwhile. To write about the hardest journey of my life and have it received by even one person is a form of healing for me.

My Friend Peter

"Most of the time I just try to rest and play with my gentle little cat in the sunlight. Nothing else is important."
(Peter)

Recently I was privileged to carry on an email correspondence with a man named Peter who is ill. The things that he said carried great resonance for me and with his permission, I am taking the liberty of sharing some of our dialogue below.

Peter: This life of ours is so short—an eye blink and it is gone. I think it is very lovely that you and your husband could hold hands together even while walking through hell. Who knows what may come? In joy or in suffering, this amazing life dazzles us all.

Vicki: You sound as if you might be ill yourself.

Peter: That's what my doctors say. I don't believe them. My little cat never gives tomorrow or yesterday a thought. Sometimes she hurts and asks for comfort. Sometimes she is tired and lies gently in the warm sun smiling up at me. What more could there be? No wonder Ramana Maharshi loved Lakshmi (his favorite cow) so very much. Lakshmi and my little cat are not going anywhere. They never have. How blessed.

Rest is greatly undervalued. It seems to me that most people in this society have not had genuine rest since they were young children. No wonder there is such unhappiness. I feel that most of the folks sitting in satsangs are really just looking for a little rest. Animals are so much smarter. They rest when they are tired. Now there's a sensible life.

It is my own experience that pain is something of an eye opener. Pain that goes on for years tends to drown out the silliness of belief systems in favor of direct contact with life, God, or whatever one wishes to call truth. Intermediaries are a waste of time when the body is crumbling. I have found that such difficulties tend to make all other sounds meaningless. Only the beating of one's own true heart has meaning.

Vicki: I wrote Pamela Wilson right after Bob was diagnosed and I clung to her "Rest and rapture, what else is there?" quote.

Peter: The person that Pamela says was her teacher (Robert Adams) took a long, slow time in dying of Parkinson's disease. I met him about a year before the end. He could barely speak and shook constantly, but his inner peace and beauty shone like a beacon. Even in the middle of a failing body he rested deeply within himself. Very lovely.

It is my own experience that suffering is what most of us do best. And much of that suffering is a result of trying to fend off strong feelings. It is my experience that nothing works anyway. In really serious illness there often is no way out. So why not do the only thing left open, which is to rest and enjoy the light sparkling on the trees. There really is nothing else. You will think I've lost it, but for me the aloneness has become a very lovely thing. I do not feel alone, as in isolated or cut off. Rather this aloneness is in a sense a powerlessness, which is very peaceful. There really is nothing I or anyone can do, so I may as well smile with my little cat in my arms and live as best I can.

As I type, that cat is asking for dinner. She is really good at being present at all times, especially at dinnertime. I think she has more wisdom in her little finger than 99.999% of all the so-called teachers out there. And talk about good-looking! Only Ramana had a face as lovely as hers.

Illness (and anything else for that matter) is beyond my or anyone's control. Sigh, I'm not very good with words. I think I'm trying to say that I have found that planning and worrying (which the mind is designed to do) go on, of course. But so what. My mind may continue to suffer, but that's not me, so let it suffer if it wants to. It is none of my concern. There is nothing it can do anyway.

Vicki: I understand how little energy you have. If I had any choice about the matter, I would just stop everything and be like your beloved cat.

Peter: I feel my friend the cat has more competence as a healer than all of these others combined. Not to mention infinitely more compassion.

Vicki: Gurus can be just as bad as doctors.

Peter: Yes. Why anyone would want to teach (as opposed to sharing) is a mystery to me. I feel that sometimes someone has an experience and thinks he is special, so he puts up a sign and advertises his services. The desperate and the frightened come, invest heavily, and eventually end up with an experience of their own, and then put up their own sign on the street. Invisible prison walls.

It has been many years since I felt a difference between guru and student, or awakened and unawakened. It is my experience that such terms have no meaning, serving only to get in the way of time spent lying in the warm sunlight with a cat in one's arms.

Note: God speaks to us in varied ways, including cats and sunlight and newfound friends. The only thing to do is listen.

The Beauty Of The Spiritual Crash

I hate to say it, but there is beauty in the spiritual crash. I am much more genuine when crashing than at any other time. Much softer and more open. Less defended. I guess that's why depth is just as important a word as height. *Little Much Afraid* in *Hinds' Feet On High Places* was led to the high places by way of the low ones. She was told to hold the hands of *Suffering* and *Sorrow* and she would not be forsaken. That is such a magical little book and very few people have ever bothered to read it. It is an allegory and I guess they are not very popular these days.

Right before I crash is when I notice myself getting harder, colder and shallower. I find myself saying hurtful things and thinking them as well. As if by coldness I can avoid the warmth within the crash. Crashes feel cold but God is near at hand. Even so, I would do anything to avoid another one.

What is a crash? For me, it is when I can no longer hold up my end of the bargain. It was this summer when I could not bring myself to go to the hospital even though Bob was at death's door. I had no power to be strong. I was humiliated, but that in itself could not enable me to push past the crash. I had to linger there for weeks and weeks.

When I am in the low places, I turn to God and to silence. I turn to honest confession that I cannot make it on my own. I need help. Once I recover, I am less apt to be as unguarded or as humble. I quickly forget my genuine needs. I gloss them over like polish on a naked nail. Yes, I am bound for the heights once again, thinking that I can get there on my own. That is human nature.

I remember working at the giant yard sale put on by Vernon Howard students every year. One woman made this comment and it reverberated in me like a bell. "We are the fallen people." Indeed. And it is just in knowing that truth that our spirits are softened and encouraged to look up. The fact of our falling is in itself a rising. It is not one that we do for ourselves, but one that is done for us. The beauty is not our own, but that of truth itself.

Last night I was lost in bad dreams. I woke up relieved to be back in the world. At some point I was walking with my old friend Jeanne from junior high. She was pregnant and I was jealous of the baby that would take all of her attention. In reality, she has third stage ovarian cancer. I am jealous of losing her to that, too.

When I read that just knowing my true nature will solve all of my problems, I recognize the Great Truth being spoken. What I do not acknowledge is those who are not living it twenty-four-seven and just talking a good game.

My friend Peter gave up on learning from others when a series of strokes delivered him from the normal world, throwing him into suffering that has continued for many years. It took him two years to learn how to crawl down the hall to use the bathroom. I am happy to say that Peter awakened naturally and on his own. He is, in his words, *bigger than the sky*. He has absolutely no interest in anything but the immediacy and the joy of existence. He yells when it hurts and cries as he is moved to do so. But it is not him, not him at all. I bow to Peter and it is totally unnecessary for me to do so (at least in Peter's eyes). He and I talk about how hard this life is. And yet he enjoys it all.

The immediacy of life cannot be denied. That is why my wall is still in place, although at times it totters, as do I. Actually, they are one thing. I know that my deepest need is to be healed of being me and for that I must wait. While I wait, I like to write. It seems to open my heart to bear witness to the chaos, the mess and the lessons. Yes, I do think that there are life lessons to be learned. They are all about learning to transcend the feeling of being separate from life. We are life itself wrapped up in a shirt that says, *I came to earth to learn my lessons and all I got was this lousy t-shirt.* The burial shroud for those who would not see.

"Every day is a new day and a new journey into myself and out again. New waters await and they often first appear as tears."
(Vicki Woodyard)

A Letter From Peter

Hello Vicki,

This life is a funny thing, isn't it? We scarcely have time to draw a breath and exhale again before it is over. All the insights, progress, and growth that we waste our precious time upon are as dust. I sit with my little cat and she purrs deep into my chest. This is life—the rest just a silly dream. I hear the doctors and the pain experts telling me I am broken. Poor dears, they do not see it is broken open. It seems we suffer because we suffer—a tautology until the sun thaws our foolish hearts.

I know Bob is so ill. It is hard to be ill. I wish it were easier for him. My poor wife suffers and the stress is sometimes very difficult for her as she sees what appears to be me have difficulty doing what was once so easy. So too, dear Vicki, must the experiences with Bob bring up so many fears for you as you are brought face to face with the unfathomable. For what it is worth, I hold your hand in this.

I have found that there is no pain when this thing that I once thought of as *me* is seen for what it is. This is such a blessing. Then even when the appearance of difficulty arises, somehow there is a sweetness behind it all. I yell and carry on, or gripe when I fall or drop things, and yet there is such a sweetness. Parts of my brain no longer work as they once did and the MRI shows loss. Ha! A brain is sooo unnecessary.

Intelligence is a light that does not need a medium to see clearly or a personhood from which to operate. It lights and lives of its own; the body is not its carrier nor its limitation. Nor is the silly little piece of imagination called a *me*. The habits wish for many things—ease for my wife, a lottery win to remove the fear of no home, and perhaps health. Ah, habits, what could we do in the presence of their absence?

Ho ho, like the ghost of a ghost we think we think and think, and think this spot of habit is us. Ha! God hugging a tree in case She falls down when She lets go. What a giggle!

Love, Peter

Note: Peter's teachings are timeless and simple, but not easy. His honesty is compelling and draws us into the immediacy and healing found in surrender.

The Imprisoned Splendor

"To know rather consists in opening out a way
Whence the imprisoned splendour may escape,
Than in effecting entry for a light
Supposed to be without."
(from *Paracelsus* by Robert Browning)

There is within each one of us a magnificent core that is waiting to be unleashed. Since the day that we were born, it has been waiting. It cannot see the light of day because it is the light of day—the Light of all Life. It is the imprisoned splendor of which the poet Robert Browning wrote.

We have only heard rumors of this light born in silence. We wonder about it. We ponder over it, but usually only when we are in the depths of despair. Surely it cannot penetrate our personal pain. But it can and by law it will—on one condition. That condition is difficult to fulfill, of course. All true conditions are difficult but divine.

The way out is in. The way of awareness is the light itself. When invited, this light of awareness is no longer imprisoned by mechanical forces and is free to fulfill its destiny. Its destiny is to do everything for us that we have been trying to do ourselves.

This is the light that never fails. It only shines into empty rooms and empty tombs, but oh, is it grand.

Better than sunset, better than rainbows, better than just about anything. It is us and now we know the great secret. We are the imprisoned splendor.

Nothing To Cling To

Dear Vicki,

I have not visited your site for a very long time, but something just now made me get up and take a look. And I saw your message about Bob being worse. Here, for what it is worth, is my own experience of this:

I went through a hell that was horrible when I first started to get so seriously ill. I lost a lot of things. Career, friends, health, loves, ability to read, and, well, more than most folks can ever imagine in their worst dreams. The hospital had said there was no hope of recovery, ever. Turning to spirituality, philosophy, learning, advaita, nondualism, etc. did not help in any way. Turning to people who said they were awake was a joke. I found nothing there that was helpful or even particularly compassionate. However I did discover one small thing that seemed to help a little—as much as possible I did my darnedest to not look to the past or the future. As the losses and suffering started to mount up, I did this with more and more intensity. And then even more. One day something died. I do not know how to say it, other than to say I no longer had a sense of a *me* at the center of things anymore, or anywhere else for that matter.

I am not sure why I am writing this to you now, or if my own experience can be of any help at all, or if it just sounds silly or a tad flakey? Yet it does seem that there is an intensity that can happen sometimes which shows us so very clearly, and yes, sometimes painfully, that there is nothing to cling to anymore.

Peter

Nobody There

The last time I looked, there was nobody there. My personality, with its labyrinthine passages and overturned furniture in its many-faceted rooms, keeps me busy from morning till night. It runs through emotions like it is practicing Shakespeare; it romps through sandboxes like so many kittens. Yet whenever I stop and look, there is nobody there. Just this awesome silence. What else can I do but tell the truth?

I have gotten up before five a.m. after a night of disturbing dreams. After being unable to go back to sleep, that thought marched into my mind, sat down and looked at me, and glared until I got up. It wanted to be entered into the computer now! So, at the risk of repeating myself, the last time I looked, there was nobody there.

My spiritual teacher used to thunder at us, "You don't exist." I never quite understood until it had ripened in my mind like a Chiquita banana. It didn't look so appealing, that yellow thought with the brown spots all over it. It smelled overripe, too, so I threw it away. Ah, there. I was back again in all my glory. But there was also fear and anxiety, the daily bread of the ego. Maybe the banana of no-self was better than it looked.

Many people have notified us of our nonexistence. That is why we try so darned hard to reinstate the illusion as quickly as possible. We don't have to try; it reboots itself automatically. It begins telling us who we are and why we must not go away. Why we must stay and mind the store. Why we must sell ourselves as product to a suspicious public. The thing is, they are doing the same thing to us.

Another principle that I have found useful over the years is this one. If something is right for me, it is right for the universe. And if it is wrong for me, the same thing applies. So I can safely do away with all this complicated thinking about how to please myself while still pleasing you. It already works that way, believe it or not. In our heart of hearts, we like for others to be as happy as we are. So now I have entered the truth into the computer and I can go back to bed. But the last time I looked, there was nobody there.

The Possibility Of Pause

Pamela Wilson's statement, "Rest and rapture, what else is there?" leads you directly into the silence if you will let it. It sums up the greatest teachings, *Be still and know that I am God.* Or as Sunyata said, "Be still and know that the *I am* is God."

The possibility of pause can give you back lost energy. When you stop to rest inwardly, the universe rests with you. You are part and parcel of the universe, so it has to work that way.

Vernon Howard says to work hard gathering energy when you have no problems. Another way to enter the silence is by putting energy money into your bank. It will always come in handy. The problem is that we save up a little energy and then spend it foolishly on a hot fudge tantrum or a shiny new quarrel we just had to get involved in. Soon our pockets are turned inside out once again.

Spirituality is about silencing thought. Someone called it quieting the roof-brain chatter. Self-remembering brings us to the simple *I am*. It is not easy to do because we have to go against our conditioning in order to let it happen.

I meditate every morning, but we should be practicing awareness all day long. It is only when we have let go that we can pause and take a giant releasing breath. Thank God there's nobody there called *me*. I forgot.

The Work Of Waking Up

The work of waking up will never be a popular thing to do. There are too many things working against it, not the least of which is our mechanical behavior. To shock oneself by throwing cold awareness into one's own face is necessary. Yes, it is a shock to see that we are not who we think we are—not at all. We think that we are a unity—that since there is one body, there must be one person inhabiting it. No, the multiplicity of the masses is inside of us. We are no different than our neighbors whom we judge and criticize for rubbing us the wrong way.

All the saints and sages attest to a state of unity, but where will we find it? Not inside our thunderous thoughts or our murderous emotions, nor in a Hallmark card or a box of popcorn, hard as we may look. So then where is unity and who is looking for it?

This question alone can lead one into greater self-understanding. The question momentarily stops the mind. It has no answer to such a question. If you stay with the mind while it is trying to think of an answer, you just may learn something that cannot be put into words or framed in a logical way. Apparently, Christ, Nisargadatta, and Ramana Maharshi were onto something when they alluded to the *I am*. Bare attention without a mantle of misperception or a scintilla of self-interest. The mind can invent answers to questions that don't deserve to be answered. They beg to be lived.

The Miasma Of Melodrama

"Mud puddles are on their way to the sea, too."

Now that Bob is back on twice-weekly chemo, every day is a potential melodrama. We get up, have breakfast, get dressed and drive to the doctor. Once there, he gets his blood drawn and if his counts are good enough, he proceeds to the Chemo Room and takes a seat. Once the nurse has accessed his port, she runs a saline solution, anti-nausea meds and the assorted chemos. I am there as an accessory.

Actually, I have time to kill and that is sometimes hard to do. I find that hard-core suffering, grief and the reality of a cancer that won't quit takes most of my energy. Oddly enough, the couple of blocks that I walk to get some lunch clears my head a little. I pass the cop directing traffic into the hospital parking lot, proceed up the cracked sidewalk and onto Peachtree Street.

Inside the franchise chicken restaurant I am enfolded in Formica, plastic and all the accoutrements of fine dining. Somehow I am always awkward eating alone. I fumble at the counter where you pick up napkins, straws and utensils. I slop a little coffee on my way to the booth. I sit there looking interested, but I am simply tired. There are always tiny dynamos of kids whirling and pushing their food away in order to play. I wish.

Once I finish lunch, I order takeout for Bob and stand at the corner waiting for the light to change. Lord knows *I* am not going to.

The Power Of Awareness

"Awareness of every reaction is your final freedom."
(Vernon Howard)

Vernon Howard is a bare-bones spiritual teacher for the ages. In his books and tapes he puts forth the ABCs of awareness in an amazing way. If you think he is too simple for you, think again. It is simplicity that sets us free. Those teachers who can transcend the mind are forever sending their messages to us if we would only listen.

They speak about awareness as the key to finding peace. Ramana Maharshi and Sri Nisargadatta are the classic advaita vedanta teachers, but Vernon Howard is an American genius when it comes to teaching the same thing. I studied him before I did the other two. When I got around to reading them, I found that Vernon Howard had already taught me about being the Self, for truth is ever-present.

The nice thing about Vernon Howard was that I could sit and listen to him in real time. As far as I know, he did nothing but speak the truth in every class he ever taught. The approach that he took was faultless; it weeded out the less serious students right away. Those who stayed got the good stuff. Ouspensky worked in the same way. He would pretend to be boring until the goof-offs left the building. Then he would scatter pearls to the remaining few. That is exactly how it should be. Those who work hard at understanding always get their reward.

I write about my path through suffering as it unfolds. Being an intuitive writer, I recognize that what Vernon Howard taught me shows through; that he is behind me as a guiding principle.

You might say that he keeps me honest. His idea of enlightenment was hard hitting; there was no one there to become enlightened. Indeed.

Enlightenment-In-A-Can

I am thinking of marketing a new product, called Enlightenment-In-A-Can. Wherever you have a bald spot in your consciousness, you just reach in and spray this product on. Once it is on, it stays on for eight hours. During this period, you can appear on talk shows telling people the secret of life.

You can sign t-shirts at bookstores everywhere, claiming that your book is in the galley stages. You can pass out mantras by the bucket-load. But at the end of the eight-hour period, you will turn back into an unenlightened one. You must drive the freeway without divine guidance, take out the trash and balance the checkbook all by yourself. Real life returns. (This insures a return trip to the can.)

I will also have focus groups for this spray-on enlightenment. They should be able to tell me what the median age is for the product. I am thinking forty-ish or fifty-ish—Visa Card-ish. You know the type. They favor shorts and sandals and carefully sculpted bodies.

I will remind them that their enlightenment will wear off in eight hours unless they get another fix. Making tapes of how to spray the product on seems mandatory. We love instructional materials, don't we? I will show them that slowly rotating the can covers every inch of bare consciousness. They will have an inner Astroturf of truth—guaranteed.

Out Of My Mind

I took my mind out of my head and unrolled it on the kitchen table. It just fit. I had been having lots of buzzing, droning thoughts and wanted to take a good look at them. First I stood up and looked and then I sat down. I could see nothing going on in there. All I saw was a pure, little mind, as innocent as the driven snow. (I love a good cliché, don't you?)

So, confident that I was imagining these pesky little thoughts, I carefully rolled the mind back up and skillfully put it back into my right ear. (I take it out on the left side and replace it on the right. I tend to be compulsive.)

I put the teakettle on and got a cup down from the rack. Should I have tea or coffee? (The mind wanted to know what the body was going to have. By this question, I knew that the buzzing was starting up again.) I told it I would have coffee and a couple of cookies. (I also knew, by answering myself, that the mind had reinstated its bifurcation as if by magic.)

The two-way dialogue was off to the races. I knew that soon I would disappear into the buzz and the emotional brouhahas that would soon begin. I would drink my coffee without tasting it and eat cookies in the same way. So discouraging. (The inner critic had arrived. It looked a little like Roger Ebert. Was it hungry? Maybe that's how I was gaining all of this weight—by feeding the multitudes, and not in a good way.)

With a total sigh, I resolved to take the mind out and examine it again. This time there were crumbs on the table and the mind recoiled as it touched bits of cookie. It was such a purist.

Nope, there was nothing on the surface of the mind. It was a still pond reflecting my body as clearly as a mirror. I smiled at its ability to do that. What a mind I had, so trusting that it mirrored anything it saw. I bowed to the purity of it and my reflection in it. As I rolled it back up and put it back through the right ear, I hoped things would go differently now.

They didn't. I could go on, good reporter that I am, to describe how often I do this. Once I went to a shrink and told him how many times a day I was taking my mind out to examine it. He said he knew I was out of my head. He tried to give me medication, but I refused. When the bill came, it was exorbitant and at the bottom he had written a personal note. *Patient is just like every other nutcase I have ever treated. What I told her seemed to go in one ear and out the other.*

Exactly!

Wave If You Love Water

"Spirituality
is like endless billboards
in the desert
announcing a desert
up ahead
without billboards"
(Jerry Katz)

Jerry's little gem led me to wonder why the sea doesn't label its waves. Or why it doesn't get a computer and take a screen shot of itself. Okay, so we humans are stuck with tasks like that. Doesn't make us entirely creative, does it. Makes us repetitive and as clingy as Saran Wrap.

If the sea doesn't bother to label its waves, why are we so concerned with the family tree? It should be a banana tree, by the way, because we are all bananas. And not top ones.

Why doesn't the wind name its own hurricanes? Is the wind so lazy it can't make time for that and it has to leave it to NOAA? Who knew the wind was so indifferent. We humans are precise, yet we are as unpredictable as the wind's storms. We have our own storms—they are called moods.

I have gotten far from the diatribe at hand. Why doesn't the sea label its waves? It must know something humans never learned—that things happen, that water makes waves that don't always wave hello.

If we are akin to waves on the ocean, can we just experience life as water and not bother to create meaningful lives as waves?

The great ones tell us we can. They tell us we can lean back and let life catch us—or not.

Schools of fish are just as smart as Harvard grads, only in a different way. They don't wear scales with designer labels or have drunken reunions to celebrate where they celebrated. When they flip people off, they don't even think about it. It comes naturally.

If I were a wave on the ocean, I would just drink it all in. An ocean is its own wet bar, after all. I wouldn't bother to pin a nametag on myself. *Hi, I'm Wave One Billion and Six.* But then again, what do I know. I'm only human.

Vicki Woodyard Waving Hello

Losing Interest In Your Story

I was talking with Peter recently about the fact that he had lost interest in his story. That is what makes him so lovable. Those of us who still believe in our personal story will continue to suffer emotionally. Joel Goldsmith healed by sitting down and turning away from the problems of his clients. So did many other healers. So I ask you, would you rather be lovable or cling to your personal story?

Peter exemplifies love, so loss of interest in the personal story can lead to deeper love. Alienation from the self often occurs precisely because we are too interested in our story. We have two choices. We can turn within and enter the silence or we can consciously turn toward life and its ongoing renewal.

My story lately has not been a pretty one, but then I am not alone in this. And there are many people who would clamor to tell me theirs. Yet if I turn away from it, lose interest in it, let the details of it atrophy, love will occupy the vacuum. Simple as that.

Peter always tells me about just sitting in the sunshine with his cat and letting her love him. There is no story going on, just this moment of pure peace. I defy you not to love a man like Peter.

The Sky—Is It Falling?
Of Course It Is.
It's Just A Matter Of Where And When.

I just bought myself a crash helmet. Now that I have it on, I will no longer be bothered by the fear of the sky falling. It's about time I got practical about it. Up until now, I have worried myself sick about the sky and it's tenuous grip on reality. And the sky doesn't give a flip about me; that much I know. It would think nothing of falling on just my house, leaving everything else intact. That is how compassionate the sky is.

I encourage all of you to get a crash helmet. I suspect you have your own fears involving the demise of your perfect little life. You may be planning an outdoor wedding or just a barbecue. If the sky falls, it will ruin the whole thing. No guru can prepare you for such an event. For that, you need a helmet.

Gurus are always telling you not to worry, to just be happy. I believe Meher Baba started that ridiculous belief. Obviously he never had the sky fall on *him*. That would have changed his philosophy. It's hard to believe in unity when the sky has taken out your skylights and blown out all of your windows. And the insurance adjuster says the sky falling is not an act of God. How dumb is that?

I used to study books about enlightenment until the sky fell on my house and now there is no house at all. The sky gave me enlightenment by taking away my house and the security it afforded. Big mistake, sky, big mistake. Because today I am wearing a crash helmet and you can't touch me anymore.

I am offering a special deal on crash helmets. One size fits all and the only color they don't come in is sky blue—I don't want to give the sky any free advertising. I also have a tree house you can time share with any or all of your buddies. If you have any brains at all, you will want to order your helmet before the sky gets wind of this and takes us all out.

Re-Entering The Sea

If you have seen the movie, *Whalerider,* you know that there is a scene where the young girl climbs upon the back of a beached whale and rides it back into the sea. "I am not afraid to die," she says (or words to that effect). As she goes underwater, you fear that she will, but she survives and becomes the leader of her tribe.

"The true you emerges when there is no attempt to prove anything to anyone."
(Vernon Kitabu Turner, *Soul Sword*)

We are a puny bunch of people these days, are we not? Riding whales into the oceanic depths is only something that people do in the movies. I have a hard time driving in traffic. But this story moved me. It is a call to spiritual warriorship. Turner writes compellingly about warriorship. "There are many ways to flow with the wind. One way is to trust yourself to be yourself."

Spirituality is that in us which is undivided; the mind cannot go beyond its element. We must trust the process of surrender if we are to go beneath the waves of sorrow and resurface with our spirit intact. I have only begun to make this journey of riding my soul back to its native home. My mind encourages me to postpone the journey. To stay and argue with people about rules and regulations, about insurance and appointments shown on the calendar. I do not have to die to honor these commitments. I can continue living a plastic life, compartmentalized and sane. But underneath the sea rages.

I have a CD by *Herding Cats* that I like. There is a line in one song about *where the black waters roll*. I can almost physically feel these black waters in my body as the song plays. I know these waters well. Don't we all? Where is our courage on any given day? Bob had to get five vials of blood drawn yesterday when he exited the trial drug study that he was on. The nurse who was drawing his blood had great difficulty in getting enough blood to come out. There were four people watching and we were all cringing. I asked him twice if he was okay, and he said that he was. Once we got home, I was able to let my hair down and feel the accumulated stress in my body.

Today we sat and meditated for a while. We talked about regaining our spirit during the next three weeks that he has off before resuming chemo once again. We have been violated by a society that values knowledge above spirit and answers above the process of questioning. It is time for us to ride the whale back into the sea.

I feel so alone in all of this. The past three years since Bob's diagnosis have been difficult. But it cannot be otherwise. This is a spiritual journey as well as a physical one. Only spirit can prove strong enough to endure what lies ahead.

In The Beginning

"Let go of regrets and reach within for the love
that you can provide for others."
(Bernie Siegel, MD)

I couldn't sleep last night. I tossed and turned and had bad dreams. I thought about many things during the hours that I lay awake and towards morning, I begin thinking about something that Bernie Siegel said to me. "God always says, 'In the beginning.' God says you should always be writing *the beginning*." So this morning, I remembered what he said and thought, *Of course*. God always returns us back to ourselves as the source of healing.

Bernie also says that when something bad happens, we are just being redirected. Again, that is a hard one to swallow when things don't turn out the way that we had hoped or planned. We spend our lives looking to the outer world for our confirmation and sadly, it can never be found there. That is why so many celebrities crack up. They look to the outer world for confirmation and they find it there. If one does not find it within, the outer will force you to return there sooner or later. The form of the outer must be broken.

I thought of the Pieta, where the mother of Jesus is holding his broken body in her arms. I suddenly understood. Our physical forms must inevitably be broken, and even though great sorrow is experienced, out of that very sorrow can come a great light. That is the way of returning home to one's heart.

Good writers are those who can break the form of their words and have the light of understanding or transcendent emotion break through. They are willing to allow their words to take second place to their meaning. They are able to strike the rock of form and have spirit shine through. In the beginning was the Word and the Word was God and the Word was with God. "In the beginning...."

Facing Challenges

Losing a child to cancer and now having a mate with it has been harrowing and challenging. Putting my pain into words is salutary for me, and perhaps for others. For we all hurt and we all face challenges.

If I were to dig deep to share one of my most painful ones, it would have to be protecting a little one from the cruelty of strangers. There was the time in the restroom of a department store when someone called my little girl a boy when her hair had fallen out from chemo, or when a child came to play with my son and he said to him, "Where's your bald headed sister?" He spit the words out cruelly, as a taunt to my already-in-pain son.

Equally as cruel were the private moments in which I would collapse by my bed and weep, crying out softly to God, "Why? What for?" He never answered. Love is silent. I would always manage to get back up off my knees, fall into bed and awaken the next morning. There was no time off for good behavior.

I remember hurriedly flying to St. Jude's on Mother's Day because my daughter had developed a throat infection. The first Christmas after her death, I sat in front of the tree crying because I had found a red rubber ball of hers under the couch.

A neighbor called and asked if I would sit with her daughter while she picked up a sick child at school. She had a doll of my daughter's that I had given to her after she died. Had I known I would have to sit and watch another child play with it, I probably wouldn't have gone. But grief is relentless and so is the inner spirit that rides it out.

For I am still here. God isn't finished with me yet, no doubt. I am not a saint, but I have been tried in the fire and bathed in grace (although usually not at the same time). I have stood by the grave of my little child, wondering that most of the graves around hers are those of small children. I think God intended that.

I am writing as much as I can about spirituality, faith, resilience and rebirth, for that is my passion. It is ironic that my passion has been placed at my weakest point. As if God were saying, "Aw, come on, I never asked you to do anything that I wouldn't do." He has allowed me to keep on keeping on, through a life of challenge and trials. Much of the trail has been uphill, so I have developed some pretty good climbing legs.

If you are going through the tough stuff in order to reach the fluff stuff, the tough stuff won't do you much good. But if you are going through it with the wish to grow, grow you will. Your sorrow will just be fertilizer for the roses that you will be stopping to smell. Your weakness will be grist for the mill and your lessons will be stepping stones to the high places. I don't regret my life, for it isn't finished by a long shot. As long as I can type into the computer, I will. So let me know if I can help you in any way.

Bigger Than The Sky

My friend Peter is having problems with energy these days and is sitting in the sunshine with his beloved cat. Peter has an uncanny ability to bypass the mind. Anything he says is total. He allows emotions to come and go, passing across the sky of his being. A laugh, a tear—all the same to him.

Obviously more intelligent than most of us, Peter has been challenged by an illness that has left him with little energy. For those of us who have been privileged to communicate with him, this makes him even dearer. His self-deprecatory emails to me are priceless.

When I told him that if I lived near him, I would come borrowing a cup of enlightenment, he just said that he didn't know anything about it, wasn't interested in it and had none to give. Yeah, right.

Peter is so candid about the frailty of his body. Yet he follows these confessions of weakness with such total empathy for the universe that you want to reach out and hug him. But he seems to be nowhere and everywhere.

His best friend is his cat (He calls himself a cat-juggler). When he speaks of sitting in the sun with his cat, he is speaking about all of us learning how to let go. I know little about the details of Peter's life. They seem not to matter to him anymore.

I suspect that talking to Peter gives one a contact high. Just what is it that he has learned through suffering? How does he transmit such wisdom in so few words? I know what he is up to. He is involving me in the paradox of peace. Shame on him. He is showing me surrender. How dare he? He is chiding me for clinging to the body. I might have known. Peter is loving me by letting me go.

Inwardly Alone

Inward honesty is reflected outwardly—or so runs the principle of the inner determining the outer. This morning I had a quiet epiphany. I saw quite clearly that my spiritual path is one of inner aloneness. I actively seek, through meditation and silence, the experience of unity, which is a form of aloneness, of all oneness. I sat there and saw, possibly for the first time, that it is good to be inwardly alone. In fact, God asks this of us.

If anyone looks within and is honest, they will see that there is no one in there but them and that they are enough. Not only enough but sufficient. "My grace is sufficient," said Christ. This is anodyne for the lonely.

I received an email last night from an old friend. She was letting me know that her brother's grandson had just died at the age of five. I would know, she said, how he felt and might want to write them a note. The phrase that came to me was that this precious child would be a rainbow on their inner landscape. Since my daughter died when she was seven, I am qualified to speak of the inner landscape. Mine remained un-peopled for years, but I was desperately looking for company, for consolation.

No more. When I can sit with silence and not fight being inwardly alone, a miracle occurs. I remember myself, that my spiritual quest is into aloneness. Often it is the inner equivalent of scaling Mount Everest. Only planting the flag of victory will do. If I succeed in planting this flag inwardly, then the outer will reflect it. I have made the two into one and the One prevails.

The Limbo Of Letting Go

I am up in the middle of the night, urged out of bed by a phrase that popped into my head—the limbo of letting go—and now this phrase has me wide awake. I can see an old broom in my mind and can see myself going lower and lower as I struggle to get underneath the broom. Is this not what our journey through life is about?

Society tells us that we must leap over the worldly hurdles of life, vaulting our way to success, but I have found the opposite to be true. God has seen to it that I have learned more by going lower than I ever have by going higher. The ego is hell-bent on leaping higher, but what does it know?

Of course the word *limbo* also means being in a state of uncertainty, which is where faith is born. One needs no faith in the sun when it is out; only in the darkness do we need faith in the light. Letting go of certainty is a wisdom we are loathe to practice.

If I told you that losing a child to cancer brought me so low that I found God, you would have no trouble believing me. If I told you that it made me no happier, would you believe that, too? God is not about making you happy. He is about making you whole. That He would do whatever it takes for this to happen is the cosmic joke and the final truth.

Wholeness ultimately is the happiest place to be, but we struggle with this for years and years. At least I did. You see, wholeness means that you must reconcile your abject cowardice with your most magnificent courage. You must balance your weak points with your God-given talents, limboing under the broom of the opposites.

When I see someone doing the limbo in my mind's eye, there is usually a crowd of onlookers clapping and cheering as you see *how low can you go.* Does this not parallel humility in the face of our daily challenges? Water seeks the lowest spot and we are the ocean.

Cancer has been a dominant theme in my life. Not mine, but my daughter's, who got it at the age of three and now my husband's. I have seen God holding out the broom and telling me to go lower on many different occasions. There was no clapping crowd, just me and an old broom of crisis. Can you go under chemo, surgery and radiation? How about death, grief and living in the absence of a beloved child? Go lower. Let go. Limbo lower now.

Letting go is easy when you realize that God is holding the broom, when you see that the God within is up to the challenge that letting go requires. For limbo is not forever, although it may seem that way.

I think that letting go requires only one thing, wholeness. And I am going to tell you how to get there immediately. Choose it. Choose heart over head, humility over height, and you will be healed by a higher power than the mind.

Hannah Hurnard wrote a spiritual classic called *Hinds' Feet On High Places.* It is about the journey of a character called *Little Much Afraid.* She sets out on the journey to the high places, called by *The Good Shepherd.* Only He doesn't seem so good to her when He asks that she learn to give love instead of seek it from others. He seems willing to sacrifice her very life for Him. But she begins her journey. He tells her to hold the hands of *Sorrow* and *Suffering*, two mysterious women who will help her on the journey.

When *Little Much Afraid* gets to the *High Places*, she has been promised a new name and that spurs her on. Ultimately after many challenges she reaches them, only to find that she must cast herself down from the very heights that she has taken such trouble to ascend. She must limbo lower now, as the musical phrase commands.

Of course, she finds that in going lower, she fulfills the purpose of her life—to serve instead of seek the high places. It is a journey of paradox and purpose. It is our journey. When will we go lower by own choice and not have it forced from us?

I am not talking about humiliation; I am talking about humility. Isn't letting go a form of humility? And yes, we will be forced to do what we do not choose consciously. That is how the game of life is played.

Maurice Nicoll, author of *Psychological Commentaries On The Teaching of Gurdjieff and Ouspensky*, was a great believer in willingness. He said if you go to something willingly, you win. Choose to go lower, instead of higher. The mysterious limbo broom can heal you of unseen arrogance and many other negativities.

Often God only talks to us when He gets us so low that we are willing to listen. Cancer often brings us to this point, as do many other life-threatening situations. Will we have the faith to live in limbo, letting go and going lower? Because God never breaks a promise to His children. "Though He slay me, yet will I trust Him." (Job 13:15).

Victory is assured when we choose humility over the ego's height. You can't think your way into wholeness; you will be broken in the attempt. Schizophrenic thinking was never meant to heal a broken heart.

These days my heart is being challenged by cancer for the second time in my life. I am honoring the old broom of limbo. Will the battle against cancer be won or lost? That is a wrong question and I am going to suggest a right one. Will the limbo take me lower than I want to go? Of course, it always does, but I know Who is holding the broom.

Blame It All On Johnny Cash

I find myself living on the edge of an abyss and often that is all there is. Me skirting the abyss as much as I can, never knowing when I might step off the edge, like the Fool in the Tarot pack. It is good to step off knowingly, but I fear the fall may kill me (She says, semi-tongue in cheek.)

Those who live on solid ground can never understand those who live teetering on the brink. I think they are the lucky ones, yet being me is the only chance I have at life. So I muddle on, always in fear, always praying to become better than I presently am.

There was a tribute to Johnny Cash on the Country Music Awards and I wept into my Scotties. There was a man who trod the edge so beautifully for us all. I never knew how sweetly one could sing from the bottom of the well. I snuffled and sank to my knees, asking God to use me before it was too late; I might not be able to get back up off the floor. But I did and as I brushed my teeth I remembered something else that made me cry.

Two little seashells named Ming and Toy. When my daughter was about five, we were at the beach and my mother was with us. She let Laurie pick out two tiny seashells at a shell shop. "Let's name them," said her grandmother. "Let's call them Ming and Toy." My daughter has been gone since 1978, but I still keep those tiny shells and look at them every now and then. More snuffles. More petitions. Blame it all on Johnny Cash.

Too Few Platelets

Bob has way too few platelets. He is getting transfusions of them, but they last about as long as snowflakes do, medically speaking. We live in a no-man's land of oncology. Up one day and down the next. Writing down the reality of it changes it somehow. I have noticed that the witness doesn't mind writing down my feelings for me. It is glad to be called since most of the time it is napping in the corner of my mind like the Maytag repairman.

Everyone wishes us well, but few call to volunteer for specific tasks. When they do, it is hard to say yes. Guilt over having to receive help—isn't that ridiculous. But the fact is that I have been on the ragged edge so long that it is wearing smooth, if you can imagine that. Perhaps it will be as smooth as the marble in the hospital lobby.

My way of resting as a caregiver is to enter the silence or to write for a while, letting the words tumble like agates in a polisher. Words like *neutropenia* and *thrombocytosis*. These are words printed out on computer sheets and handed to us after Bob's labs are done. I look at them and file them with the stack of others. His file is so thick that the doctor ordered the nurse to thin it down. It is tattered around the edges just like my soul.

Tonight I am going to bed on time and getting up early as usual. At noon we will be at the Infusion Center getting Bob those platelets and then I will write some more. The eyes of the Maharshi are glowing with peace. He knew cancer and he also knew peace. A model for us to aspire to—a place to lay our head—a whisper of reassurance that God will wipe away the tears and give us peace.

The Saint

Lately, things have been taking turns for the worse. I find myself driving in traffic to the hospital several times a week so that Bob can get blood and platelets. Each time we go, it requires a gathering up of tote bag items that will get us through the next several hours. I am a glorified bag lady.

My spiritual practice has grown very one-pointed. Karma yoga practiced in an intense inner fire. Who's to say what I am learning? My spouse has his own lessons going on and everyone applauds his courage. Our relationship is becoming a thin shell of what it used to be. There is less talk as he loses ground to the cancer. We go about our business in silence much of the time.

Today I met a kitchen saint named Cora Campbell. She is in charge of the baked goods at the hospital cafeteria. I had read about her in the newspaper, about how physicians praised her corn muffins and how everyone who knew her loved her. Well, today, there she was, standing by her muffins and yeast rolls. I got to give her a big old hug and say "thank you." She said that people asked her why she didn't want to retire. "I tell 'em everyone would miss me," she smiled. Of course they would.

Bob sat in the chemo chair eating her turkey pie out of a styrofoam container. He is so thin that his pants are folding over at the waist. His knuckles are dry and bleeding. It is all he can do to keep his balance as he walks. I told him about meeting Cora Campbell and he was so pleased. Who's the saint here, anyway?

My Body

This morning I had a physical therapy session for my neck. The therapist, Kent, was taking me through my range of motions and we were getting to know each other. Like Bernie Siegel, he has a shaven head. I told him what Bernie said about why he shaved his head—to bare his emotions, spirituality and love.

Kent commented that when he told me to let go, I wasn't able to do so. "A lot of times," he said, "people will be telling me one thing and their body will be telling me something else. And that's where the rubber meets the road."

I have known for a long time that I am unable to let go. But knowing and doing are far removed. It is good to know where you need to do more work—at not working. I say that tongue-in-cheek and also in truth. Without descent into the depths, we will never ascend to the inner heights. That's just how it is.

Bernie had asked me what my pain in the neck was about. I honestly cannot put it into words, so I am putting it into my body. But I am good at words, if nothing else, so I will try. I need to be embraced, not braced. Bracing myself against emotional pain hurts my body. I write a lot about letting go. Bernie says that you teach what you need to learn.

Those of you who resonate to what I write know that we are all in the same boat. We are each other. We mirror each other. Thank God that this is true. Sometimes we can all be a pain in the neck and what we really need is to embrace and be embraced. It seems the logical thing to do, but how hard it is to stay open, to contain the pain. The body can be an alchemical vessel if we allow it to be. We can let the pain remain, embracing it with our own higher consciousness. I know this, but not all of the time.

I would like to say a word to my body, "I am sorry that I have allowed you to get so tense and in such pain. Forgive me. I am getting you some help. Thank you for all that you do." My body doesn't speak in words, but I saw the tears in its eyes. We will be okay.

Inevitability

There is an inevitability to life that is downright frightening. It will happen 24/7. And right alongside that is the accompanying truth. It will end finally. This double-bind causes us to live in fear and dread. Nothing wrong with admitting this because that is just how the game is rigged. We are playing on the field of opposites, in time. All true spiritual work is about seeing this and calling on something outside of ourselves to help us.

The ego is preoccupied with itself, but no one else is. That should be a tip-off right there. Generally, no one is obsessing over us but us. Now and then someone becomes famous and is ruined by others obsessing over them. This proves that fame is a real downer. Living in Tao and being unknown is what all those little Zen masters were about. They were happy to watch a frog go *ker-plop*.

Every day I face the inevitability of Bob's cancer. And the fact that it will cease to be. And that my life will change. And that I may not have the courage to go on. That is what my life is about right now. Other things are happening right under my nose, but I don't see them or welcome them necessarily.

My friend Peter faces the inevitability of his illness but he has come to have a different view. Because he focuses on the beauty of now he has become "bigger than the sky." I hasten to say that it just happened to Peter and in the happening, he seems to have disappeared. This erasing of the personal has allowed him to become a channel of love, at least for me. Such is the inevitability of spiritual law. Letting go leads to grace.

That Chair

My friend Jeanne has just had surgery for ovarian cancer. I am weeping as I write. Her husband, Joe, is such a dear. "I like being a caregiver," he said, "but I am going to have to let Jeanne tell me what she wants."

"What do you mean?" I asked.

"Well," he said, "For instance, there was a chair in the hospital room and before she tried to get out of bed, I wanted to move it out of the way for her. She said, "If I haven't tripped over it yet, I'm not going to trip over it now."

Jeanne can always make me laugh. She told me before going into the surgery that she was going to fight for her life. She has had breast cancer twice and been cancer-free for over twenty years. We went to junior high school together and were best friends. We reunited this summer; not having seen each other in some forty-odd years. "Maybe we can be friends in our old age," she said.

"Do we have to have matching notebooks?" I asked her.

"Only if I get to pick them out," she said. It was a reunion made in heaven. She said that she would be here for me as I went through Bob's cancer. More tears. Like that chair, I am just going to let them be there.

I just got the call. Jeanne died this morning after a long battle against her cancer. I wept tears coming from the deepest place inside of me—the place where junior high school friends become what they now call BFFs, best friends forever.

Jeanne always did it her way. As I wept into the phone, Joe told me that she wanted her ashes to be scattered in the backyard. At her memorial service there will be songs from the old Methodist hymnal she loved so much.

I told my son the news and these were my thoughts about my friend Jeanne. She spoke from her heart, which is a rare gift. She lived with boldness and was one of the most sentimental people I have ever met. She celebrated eccentricity and thrived on the truth.

Each life gifts itself back to the earth when its cycle is complete. As my friend Lorin Roche says, "The earth takes dead bodies and makes trees and flowers out of them." Jeanne knew that.

ICU

This summer Bob ended up in the ICU for a few days. I had been working on a manuscript and finally got it in shape to submit to a university press. I was very hopeful about it, as the editor had said he liked my work very much.

I got up one morning determined to mail the manuscript no matter what. Bob had been feeling especially bad the last few days. But by this time I was so used to one crisis following another that I decided to put the manuscript first, no matter what. I mailed it and it was downhill from there. When I got home, his condition had worsened. He was having trouble breathing. Our son and I drove him to the oncologist's office. They quickly determined that he was not getting enough oxygen.

Before I knew it, I was following the doctor, who was running behind a nurse pushing a wheelchair with Bob in it. He had an oxygen mask on and we were racing to the ICU. Within a day they had him stabilized, but he stayed in ICU for about three days. Here, he fell back into paranoia like he had after his bad drug trip. Paranoia is common in ICU patients.

The love returned as well. He would call me several times an hour to tell me how much he loved me. My love for him was boundless, but I was tempted to disconnect the phone.

The guilt I felt about putting myself before him was real. Who did I think I was? Was his ICU visit just my bad karma boomeranging on me? Could be. Was I really bothered? No, I was learning how little I knew about love. When you are breaking, all you can do is breathe.

A Relationship

I seldom write about the personal relationship between my husband and me. It is no different than anyone else's, yet it is a snowflake relationship like all others are, too. He claims to have fallen in love with me when he saw me coming down the steps of our grammar school. I was wearing a red skirt and a white blouse and he said I looked like an angel. I paid him no notice until high school when we began dating. He went away to Georgia Tech and I stayed home and went to our local college in Memphis, Tennessee. We married right after he graduated and that was a while ago.

I have always depended on him. He taught me how to drive, which was a big mistake as I never became a good driver. But that is not the point of this piece. I started out to talk about our relationship. It is complicated and simple, like all relationships are. Since he has been sick, the relationship has been thrown into reverse. I have to experience my strengths and he his weaknesses. Before, it was the other way around.

Today we sat in the silence for almost an hour—meditating. It felt so good we did it again later in the day. In between, we went out to eat. When we came back, we watched part of *Joseph Campbell and The Power of Myth* on PBS. "You know," I said to Bob, "our sitting in silence is what he was talking about—experiencing the transcendence." Yes.

Our hearts are vulnerable from the daily pain of his cancer. We admit that, but he tends to be stoic and I emotional. Since we grew up in the same neighborhood, we reminisced a lot the past couple of years. We talk about what we liked to eat and where, for instance. Memories of Krystal hamburgers on the train to

Jackson, Mississippi to visit his grandmother come to his mind. I talk about the way my grandmother fried chicken in her old iron skillet.

Our relationship is sacred space. We squabble and nag each other. I say too much and he says too little. He is genial and I am quiet and aloof. I used to be a dancer and he used to play basketball. These days he can barely walk and yet he never complains. It is the relationship that must have the wings.

He never tells me I look nice on any given day and yet he is proud of me overall. I respect him totally, but he gets on my nerves from time to time. That is not what matters. What matters is the transcendence that Joe Campbell speaks about. It is capable of turning the marriage into an instrument capable of making music when it could have made only noise.

I Could Tell You...

I saw a counselor last week. Bob was clearly in the last stages of his disease and my grieving was suddenly like post traumatic stress disorder. I knew what lay ahead. So I sat in his office filled with plants and lovely things talking of death and falling apart. Before the therapist dove into the mess with me, he encouraged me to tell him a bit about myself.

"I am shy," I said, trying to introduce my neurosis boldly, trying to be upfront about my occasional panic attacks.

"You've got a web page where you put it all down for the whole world to see and you're shy?" He said words to that effect.

In my own mind I am shy because I am an introvert. However, as a writer I like to share my feelings in the most honest way that I can. They are raw-boned teenagers who can't seem to get enough spaghetti and meatballs. They eat over the sink and clean out the fridge in a New York minute. These gangly emotions of mine are uncontrollable. On my website I give them their space and let them speak. Then they take the car and leave me alone in the house and grief drifts in the windows.

I let my grief speak, telling about cancer and using words like *incurable* and *heartache,* because they are part and parcel of what make me as a writer. It is true that I know peace, but it is so quiet and gentle that it seldom gets the space that it is due. Like a kitten, it is content to play in a paper bag and go unnoticed as it naps on the TV.

I like to share what my heart is experiencing because someone is going through pain and suffering, too. Maybe I speak for all of us when I write the raw-boned stuff; I don't know. For instance, Thursday his oncologist told him that the chemo is no longer working and that the new experimental drug would be a good idea. I could go further and tell you that the myeloma is knocking at the door and there is no substance strong enough to keep it out.

I could tell you that we have been married for thirty-seven years and are measuring our life by a different standard these days. What is it? I am not sure that I even know. But the old one of enough money in the bank and places to visit and things to do is breaking down. That's a good thing.

Catch Me When I Fall

If we are all part of the universal consciousness, will it catch me when I fall? When friends wrote letters to my husband, he wept. This is not something that he does very often, but I think he felt the net had been put in place and that he could fall. How often do we trust that this will be so? Does it take years of suffering before we admit our fragile state of existence in this temporary world, the relative world, as the Sufis call it.

"My strength is made perfect in weakness," says the Christ-consciousness. Does our very weakness comprise the net in which we can fall? I remember my brother telling me, many years ago, to lean back and let God catch me. I was flying to Europe with my husband, my first and only time to do that, and I was very anxious. I tried to do what he said, but my own effort blocked the ease I so badly needed. The ego is a fortress of pain constructed of thought. That is the human predicament.

Zen teachings point us to the truth that all of life is suffering. I can attest to that. But conscious suffering can free us from mechanical suffering. When we remember that we are all one, the net of unity becomes strong enough to catch us. All we really want is to let go.

As my husband's illness requires more and more of me, I get more and more exhausted. Does the physical body know how to rest if we have the sense to allow it plenty of time to do so? Do the emotions have the wisdom to quiet down and contemplate peace. No. Only awareness of something higher can dissolve the dissatisfaction. Only light can relax us while we are struggling in the dark.

As I walk the spiritual path carrying my daily burdens, I forget that I can release them and just sit down and rest. My mind blocks out this vital truth and before I know it, I am exhausted. That is why a good strong spiritual practice takes tending. It requires as much attention as a growing child. It must be fed far more than three times a day. Sometimes it will wake you up at night and ask you to soothe it. But why, I think. It is supposed to soothe me. But the opposites are not that easily figured out. I find that paying attention to my pain in the right way helps to disperse it. Go figure.

At the very end of the path is a light—that I have heard. I have also heard that it is at the very beginning and at all points in-between. I have also heard it rumored that we are the path, the light and each other. It's a good thing that we can fall into that net when we choose to do so. Is it in the mind or in the spirit? As we ask ourselves this question, it is good to know that there is no answer, that we are the answer and that is why we cannot be told. We must be one with the question, that is all. That is the net that can hold us.

Heavy Grace

Ram Dass speaks of suffering as *heavy grace*. Amen to that. The grace of this day has all but floored me. Not only is Bob anemic and in need of transfusions, but he also needs platelets. It was only a couple of weeks ago that our neighbor who is a physician said he could have a *bleed* that could prove to be fatal.

We stumbled over to the cafeteria and ate in silence and then I walked him to the Outpatient Infusion Center. I drove home listening to the radio and checked the mail and the computer.

Now that I have the freedom of privacy, I can let down my hair and cry. If what I am recounting sounds familiar, that's because it is. I have written in this vein as often as his have been hooked up to IV machines. It never gets any easier; in fact, the fatigue level rises daily. I am pretty much wiped out.

Today I spoke with the social worker in the doctor's office and she, as always, gave me plenty of space to feel my grief and helplessness. Sometimes a nod is enough as the story spills out into tears and remorseful words. Why can't I be stronger and less me. I tend to say things I regret and build walls around myself. Of course these tactics don't work. All they do is isolate me.

Writing is confessional for me. For those of you who don't know me, I write about my husband's battle with multiple myeloma. For those of you who know me even better, I am writing about myself. Occasionally I rise above conditions and words roll in like a mist, unfurling like so many fronds on a fern. That is grace.

Today

Today was altogether too familiar. It began early in the morning at the surgeon's office. We had never met him and he was very nice. He seemed to think that Bob's gall bladder surgery might better be postponed for at least a week, although he understood the urgent need for him getting back on chemo. He said, "I'll put in a call to your doctor and see how he feels about it." We sat in his office for far too long, only to have him send us up one floor to see Bob's doctor. We understood that he would "just have a word with us" about when to do the surgery.

About three hours later he worked us in, after we had made a co-pay. (We thought it was just a pop-in visit). I did get a chance to speak to the social worker in his office. She understood that I was at the breaking point. "Can you just put a pillow over your head and wail?" she asked me.

In shuddering sobs I told Bob to stop asking me to do things. This is how ugly a cancer experience can be. Sitting in the hospital cafeteria at 2:30 in the afternoon eating a sandwich and facing the pre-admission procedures after you get through. Coming home to crash. Knowing that three days later there will be surgery and then more chemo.

His doctor wants him to have the surgery this week because the cancer is on the march. Goody. Bring a straitjacket and we will all have tea. I told the social worker that I was out of strength, perspective and in need of help myself. Never mind the cancer patient. All of my spiritual knowing has evaporated and that is just how it is.

Now is not the time to wax poetic about the Eternal Now. The infernal chaos of cancer is making me dance to its tune. I always try to tell the truth, even when it hurts. And hoo boy, is it hurting.

At pre-admission I looked at people in wheelchairs and with casts. I took the familiar walk to the coffee machine that has decent brew and asked myself why. Why does a chicken cross the road? What are all of these people saying to each other on their cell phones? Pick up a loaf of bread on your way home? Where is home and for goodness sake, who is hungry anyway?

Losing It

Lately I have been losing it. My husband's surgery to remove his gall bladder kicked off my latest round of raw reactions. It exacerbated my already low tolerance for suffering. If the world is a mirror, I find it to be cracked!

I have reached out my heart to find understanding. Wet with tears, I have asked others to shower me in grace. I stayed home from the hospital because I just couldn't go. I needed to stay home and lick my paws and sleep in my kennel. I am not running with the wolves but panting with the puppies.

Kindnesses have been kibble for me and I have taken to licking the hands of complete strangers. I feel like I have fleas though because I keep chasing my tail.

Writing is my therapy and so I must put my paws on the keyboard and type nonsense. There is an endorphin release on its way. After posting a silly piece, I feel like running around the house in circles. Then I fall exhausted in a heap and chase rabbits.

If you like the nonsensical approach to life, I will let you come over and walk me. Keep in mind that I have not been spayed and am afraid of cats.

We Shall Go On...

A friend writes to say that she feels for me as I reel from yet more bad news about Bob. I sit in front of the computer, free to cry at last. I feel my heart as a sliver of ice in my cold body. I have spent the day trying to get in touch with something, anything that will resonate as a way out. I remember being told that all of my teacher's true students would be broken and thrown back on themselves.

Oh God, I am not strong enough. I can write, I can joke, but I cannot cure my own heartache. The irony is that I know that nothing will take it away. I would choose insanity if I could, but choice has nothing to do with things like that. My teacher said, "When you are carrying your cross up Crucifixion Hill, offer no resistance whatever."

Bob and I ate soy corn dogs from a box and an apple and yogurt salad for supper. People have to eat. In spite of the cancer, our life is very normal. I like neatening things up and going to bed with everything in order. I write about spirituality and that is just a part of who I am. I am also an introvert who doesn't let anyone in but the few.

I know the great secret taught by all mystics—there is only everything. Like a child with attention deficit disorder, I forget that illusion hurts big time. I try to take care of things that are just mirages in the desert of my mind. I am riding a camel to water that doesn't exist, but then, neither do I.

My biggest treasure is my marriage and that is why it is being put to such a test. Bob is stronger than most people because he has such a pure heart. The old line, *His strength was as the strength of ten because his heart was pure*, seems very true to me. I have done my utmost to take care of him for the past three years and I have grown a lot. But this little sliver in my body hurts like hell. Maybe when it is completely gone I will be different, but not today.

Multiple myeloma is a devastating disease, an ugly blight on the body's ecosystem. It is ravaging Bob in its own sweet way and I am going along for the ride. Perhaps some of you can relate, having lost a loved one to cancer. It has happened to me twice and my spirituality has been cracked, twisted and melted down many times over. Some days I reach the silence and drink it in like water from a crystalline spring. That is enough for me. I need no carnival entertainment or four-course dinners, just the peace of letting go—and then going on some more.

My friend Peter is undergoing his own torment; his doctors suspect that he is having many small seizures every day. Yet he encourages me by talk of watching the wind in the trees and feeling it on his skin. I love him like a brother and we only know each other through the Internet.

I lean my face against the monitor as if to gather some of his wry wisdom. We shall both go on, filing reports from the front, embedded reporters in the war against pain. If our reports make people uncomfortable, perhaps they are in need of a good cry themselves. There is no going to commercial in such a report, however. Someone has paid the price for all of this and one day we will be free. Until then, we talk and write and witness.

Sitting With The Teacher

I have been sitting with the teacher for a while now. It all began when Bob was admitted to the ICU and is continuing. I remember how Irina Tweedie, author of *Daughter of Fire*, sat with her guru, Bhai Sahib, both of them ill and in the mystery. She would storm and rage and pray and he would exemplify the stoic.

I find that learning from my husband's cancer is as awful and demanding as sitting with the guru. Putting Boost in the blender with Ovaltine and drinking from it like it was going to put some courage on me—no, just extra pounds.

What can I convey that does not sound trite and self-pitying? I just try and hit the highlights of what is going on in the depths of my soul. I lay down on the bed and Bob wanders in.

"There's something on the bedspread; your shoes are dirty," he says. Sure enough, I have tracked in mud. Deja vu. Four years ago it was dog doody, so I have made some progress.

Kwan Yin, Goddess of Mercy and Compassion, manifests in the form of a male nurse who offers anything, but anything that you need. When I asked for coffee, he rode down with me in the elevator to show me where the best hospital coffee could be found. A machine that even made espresso. Ah, so good, better than Boost.

I am unveiling myself, unwrapping the grave clothes, the swaddling bands. Who lies within this cocoon of heavy grace, as Ram Dass calls his suffering. Does she know what is going on? Will she speak when she gets ready? Or will she be like

Sleeping Beauty and fall right back into the earthly dream? I pray for her as I would a little child.

ER

ER. Two lettered hell. It began on Monday when Bob was driving to the doctor who is administering his trial drug. In the parking lot he blacked out at the wheel and hit a car in front of him. Unhurt, he saw the doctor, who checked his heart and it sounded okay. At the kitchen table later that night he tumbled from the chair unconscious. My son told me to call 911 and the EMTs were there in a flash. Two kind men examined Bob and left it up to him whether or not he would go the ER. He thought he might have broken a rib, so my son and I went with him. He had a third seizure there and luckily the doctor caught it.

"Temporal lobe seizure," he said. Dilantin was ordered and a battery of tests. You see, taking a trial drug for cancer has its downside. But then so does multiple myeloma. The X-rays of his ribs were displayed in the examining room. The doctor grinned wryly, "You've broken all of your ribs," he said. Not really, that was done by the disease.

The next day I came down with a virus, but managed to get Bob home. Lordy, lordy, lordy. When it rains it pours. Sometimes the vichara, "Who am I?" becomes, "Why, me, Lord?" Curiously, I have stayed calm, as if reacting would put me over the top. There are more lines for me to read in this curious script and that's the truth. Sometimes I forget them and have to improvise. Or dig deep to find an old emotion that I can call on—you know, the Actor's Studio.

The doctors have their lines down pat and emotionlessly delivered. (I know a secret. They are not really doctors. They are just playing one on Planet Earth.) They have forgotten this, as most of us do. They seem to have forgotten that we have brains as well, although our bodies seem simple enough for them to master. They knock us in the knee and elbow, poke our bellies and shake their heads. Who are they kidding? They are *playing* doctor.

Coming home from the hospital seems to shine the light on all of the cobwebs and loneliness that you left behind and hadn't noticed. The first night that I came home alone, the rooms reeked of my long-term pain. Who have I become and why? The only thing to do is put the kettle on and mindlessly eat cookies. My computer keys record the oddest things, like "I am getting older," and "Who really loves me, I mean *really* loves me?" Two people on the planet. My husband and son. Not enough, not nearly enough. "Who do *I* love?" seems to be a fair question. Those two tall and kindly men. Men who are saying a long goodbye. It's tough; it's very, very tough.

Chunks Of Me Are Falling Into The Sea

Lately I feel like a giant iceberg making my way through northern seas. Something ominous is out there and I am rudderless and heavy, drifting silently into darkness. A feeling of foreboding looms.

Bob has been looking pale and he is scheduled for chemo this morning. I fix us oatmeal with extra raisins, fortifying us against the formless fear of cancer out of remission. The wooden spoon stirs the heavy oatmeal in the stainless steel pan.

Bob puts on a yellow shirt and I don't like the way his skin matches its pallor. But we get in the car and go. In the oncologist's waiting room we see lots of people just like us. Patients and caregivers waiting their turn. Pieces of conversation drift into my ear and none make any real sense. I don't know these people, but we are kin. Some smile, but no one really meets. In the chemo room it will be different. Being hooked up to IV's for long hours breeds solidarity. But now we are waiting.

Bob's name is called and he goes to get his blood work done. Fifteen minutes later I join him in the chemo room. It is the weekend before Easter and every chair is taken. As if people wanted to get the hard stuff out of the way before celebrating.

A glitch happens. The chemo nurse comes and tells us that Bob's doctor wants to delay his chemo for a week and have him get two units of blood instead. His hemoglobin is far too low. She suggests that we go get a bite to eat and be at the Infusion Center at one o'clock.

The cafeteria smells like hospital and fried chicken. We eat something to sustain us and wend our way to the Infusion Center. We haven't been there before. After filling out the usual forms, we are told that the blood has not arrived. If I had known that it would not get there until three o'clock, we would have gone home and taken a nap. I leave Bob and go home alone. I will send our son to pick him up around eight o'clock, when he will be finished.

As I lie down I remember several things for which to be thankful. The nurses at the Infusion Center were kind. Bob is getting help. I found the car. I remembered that I was drifting through life asleep to my pain. The iceberg of the ego is deadly dangerous, as dangerous as any cancer. It can upend ships carrying precious cargo. I know. I have lost relationships to the ego. If I lose my husband to cancer, I will never lose him in this way. We have told our secrets and our stories to each other as we have gone through this ordeal. Chunks of our egos are breaking off and floating away. It's about time.

Normally, the ego likes being an iceberg in the waters of life. It can move slowly and stealthily into things, crushing them by its weight of negativity. This morning I woke up briefly and knew that I was headed toward dangerous waters. Not my husband's need to be transfused, but by my own need to receive conscious life. Thank God I can fall into the sea. Chunk by chunk I can fall away from myself. And one day there will be only sea. And I will be free.

Forget Rumi

Each day brings its share of stress. Today Bob got his CBC taken and he is holding his own, but barely. The chemo nurse said he could probably go without a transfusion this week. We drove to the OK Cafe and it was just 10:45. We had already eaten breakfast and they weren't serving lunch yet. I finally ordered coffee cake and Bob wanted biscuits and grits. Time passed and the waitress returned. "Sorry, but we're out of biscuits." We looked at each other and knew that it was time to hit the road. So we did.

When we got home, the water department was trenching out the road in front of our driveway to lay new pipe. We pulled over and waited about ten minutes for them to finish so we could pull into the drive. Turning on the news, I saw that a threatened suicide was on a bridge near our house and tying up traffic on the interstate for miles. Maybe it was a good thing we didn't stay for lunch.

This afternoon I watched Sharon Stone on Oprah. She talked about her white light experience and the fact that death is immediately beside life, or something to that effect. I am seeing this up close and personal, as she did when she had her aneurysm. I don't doubt her for a minute.

If life has anything to teach us, it is inexorability. When I suffer, there must be no desire to escape it or it will just stay longer. The pearl in the oyster of my life is wisdom. I vow I get high on the way things work out on the spiritual level. The man fell from the bridge, but he did not die. I am cooking chicken for dinner and Bob is taking a nap. As I have said before, forget Rumi. Pay attention to your own miracles.

The Marriage Blanket

The social worker in the oncologist's office spoke of the marriage blanket today. She said I needed hope and I confessed that the only hope I had was for my husband to live. She looked at me wisely and kindly. "Perhaps you need to look at the blanket that you have woven together and begin to separate the strands." I am not sure what she meant.

We ate lunch quietly and I tried to talk about death with Bob. The people at the other table were quiet and all the other tables were empty, as it was well past the lunch hour. I said that we needed to talk about whatever made us cry—that it would lighten the load. When we got home, Bob took a rest and I laid down beside him and begin to weep. I went upstairs to the guest room and lay there crying. The strands that are my responsibility to unweave, what are they and where do I find them? Can they be identified with any certainty? I know that I am angry with all of this suffering. I can't take much more.

I came back downstairs and laid on the bed with Bob. As he looked out the sliding glass door, he saw something. He got up and said, "There's a cardinal in the squirrel trap!" He had set the trap the day before. We always drive the squirrels to the river and set them free, but today it was a beautiful redbird.

"Wait a minute," I said, "You don't need to be doing that. I'll come and let the bird go." The poor cardinal flapped around in a daze. I opened the door and he flew away. It didn't hit me until I sat down at the computer to write this. If life is a metaphor, it had just spoken to both of us. Can we be grateful for that which sets us free? That is a question that I am loathe to answer.

Arunachala

Come with me to Arunachala, the holy hill of Piedmont Hospital, and into the parking garage. Go with me in my car as I drive up to the third deck, park and walk down the steps and into the 95 Building where the oncologist is located. Step into the elevator and ride with me to the fifth floor. Sit with me while Bob and I wait to see what his labs are today. Not so hot. His doctor is summoned and decides that today he shall have thirteen bottles of IVIG by IV, two units of blood tomorrow and thirteen more bottles of IVIG the following day.

Come with me to the hospital cafeteria where I eat a plate of chicken and mashed potatoes, washed down with a cup of coffee. As I go back through the line and order food to take back to the fifth floor for Bob. As I ask the nurse if she minds putting it in the microwave in the staff lounge. (Thy rod and Thy staff, they comfort me).

Be with me as I drive home, check my email and tell our son that his dad needs IVIG again. Watch out, because I am about ready to blow—just kidding. No, I just write as I am led to write. The holy hill today seems to be not Arunachala, but wherever I have to circuitously travel. Does that make me religious? Hardly. Does it make me strong? No, weaker than ever. Does it make me crazy? Undoubtedly. Does it break my heart? Of course. Of course.

Friday nights are somehow difficult for me. The week has come to an end, but my tension has built. I eat mindlessly and sit in front of the TV. Books are by my side, but I prefer to watch Comedy Central. It is soothing in the way that eating chocolate is. It does you no good, but Friday night is not for healthful therapy, now is it?

I got a massage today and found myself rising above my horrible week with Bob. His platelets fell to an all-time low and he had to get tanked back up. I was able to access all the wrong emotions and use them to the fullest. Self-pity waxing like the new moon. Geez, it just doesn't let up for us. But I let myself be worked on diligently by a skilled masseuse who came to the house. We were in the zone, spiritually speaking. The silence was a shared respite for us.

Writing offers me respite as well. Words arriving just in time to fill the computer screen. Where do they come from and why am I unconsciously selecting the ones that I do? It's like playing ping pong with yourself. Ping...pong...ping...pong. The net divides the conscious from the subconscious. Ping...pong...words crossing back and forth between different parts of myself. Awesome.

Somewhere in between the ping and the pong I reside. I reached into the bottom of a Graeter's ice cream carton, scooping out the last slabs of rich, dark chocolate. That is as close to home as it gets. Bittersweet, but unbelievably good. I reluctantly tossed the carton in the trash. If it had had arms and legs I would have embraced it. Such is the nature of escape on a Friday night.

Permission To Go

Bob was in the hospital for what might be the last time. I only knew that I was as weary as I had ever been. The chaplain turned up one morning to visit him; that hadn't happened before. He was a burly man in a tweed jacket with a rumpled, comforting look. I liked him immediately.

He visited with us and when he said a prayer, he invited me to look him up in his office if I felt the need. I knew I wanted to do that.

So I wended my way through the hospital's maze of corridors, ending up lost on the ground floor where his office was located.

"I'm looking for the chaplain's office," I said, collaring a cafeteria worker as he came into the hallway bearing a tray.

"I'll lead you there," he said with a generous and sympathetic smile. I am sure I was telegraphing panic and he could do no less.

I entered the chaplain's office and told his secretary I wanted to speak with him.

"He's not in right now," she said and I knew he was indeed in his office, but with no plans for a conference right at the lunch hour. Suddenly he walked out to speak with her and I caught him. So he agreed to give me a few minutes.

"Your husband is staying alive to take care of you," he told me.

I looked at him wordlessly.

"He is hanging on—for you." The rest of what he said escapes my memory.

I left his office on a mission. I miraculously found my way back to Bob's room. Once inside, the words came tumbling out.

"You don't need to stay alive for my sake. I can take care of myself." Six little words that said, in effect, I am stronger than I think I am. Bob looked at me from his hospital bed and took my hand. I wept. He lay in silence. But I am sure the light shone down on us both. Eternity often gives us a glimpse of how love endures.

Stopping Treatment

Treatment has stopped. We were called into the oncologist's office where he sat soberly with his nurse at his side. As I recall, the words went something like this:

"Bob, we think it's time to stop treatment for your own good. The transfusions just aren't working any longer. We can get you into hospice care and you won't have to suffer through any unnecessary procedures any longer."

When the day comes, somehow you are ready. At least I was. Bob had become increasingly weak. My son and I were breaking under the strain. We knew it was a matter of weeks. But Bob wasn't ready to give up. It just wasn't his nature.

Driving home, I said, "You know he is right—don't you?" My words felt false and futile. I was beyond feeling much of anything but sheer exhaustion. Frankly, love doesn't have anything to do but BE. And so we were together in silence.

The nurse had told me that once the transfusions stopped, Bob would not live more than a week or so. And now we took care of him at home for a few days. He was using a walker to move from bed to bathroom to kitchen. I still remember the sound of him coming down the hall with it.

He fell in the bathroom one night. I had taken a sleeping pill and was oblivious to what happened. My son only told me about it later. "I heard Dad calling me from the bathroom. I couldn't get the door open all the way because he was leaning against it. I inched my way in and he sat there on the tile."

"I think I know what to do," Bob said, always the engineer. "Get a screwdriver and take the door off the hinges. Put me on a sheet and you can drag me back to bed." And that is what happened while I slept.

The hospice worker came to make an assessment of his condition. "He is very weak," he said, speaking to me as I sat beside the bed. "I can arrange for him to be admitted tomorrow."

Later that night was when Bob began to hallucinate, but happily and peacefully. He saw things in the picture hanging over the bedroom fireplace. He wanted to show us trucks coming around the mountain in the picture. He saw the chrome and the logo on one. Things like that keep one focused on the humor rather than the gathering darkness.

I remember when Bob was in ICU, I got dressed to go to the hospital. I was crashed, smashed and dashed. I had nothing left to give. At this point I needed to be receiving love and not trying to dredge up one more spoonful of it.

I opened the door to leave and a wasp flew into my throat and stung it. I retreated. Decided that it had a message for me. The next day I got five minutes down the road on the way to the hospital and the road was closed. Again, I came home. Bob was in the hospital and I looked like I should be. No easier way to say it. I was on my last legs.

When he had his gall bladder removed, a nurse walked beside him into the prep room. He fell down and they took him to X-ray before they would operate on him. There were no broken bones, in his knees at least, so they performed the surgery. I knew that was a mistake.

My son was with him during the surgery; I couldn't go. That is when I curled up on a ball and waited by the phone. Sure enough, at midnight, the phone rang.

"Mrs. Woodyard, this is Dr. Smith, "We need to take your husband back into surgery. He's bleeding at the incision site. He bled everywhere we touched him. He is a very, very sick man."

Miraculously, Bob had a two-month rally after that. This marriage of ours, which began in heaven, had descended into hell. It wouldn't have mattered to me if you had served me a round of roast beef and a glass of expensive champagne. If you had dressed me in diamonds or flown me to Paris for the weekend, it wouldn't have mattered. All that mattered was that the suffering ended. It had gone on for almost five years. It was time for the transition.

Into The Light

Bob was admitted to hospice on December 16 and spent four days there before leaving us on December 20, 2004. It was cold and windy the entire time. My heart was leaden and did not know Christmas was looming. We drove there in an ambulance and Bob was too weak to protest at all. Emaciated and moving in and out of rationality, he was in little or no pain. That was left to my son and I, who were facing his final days. In his room was a small Christmas tree complete with tinsel and ornaments. It was as unreal as everything else.

My sister, Laurie, had driven straight through from Williamsport, Pennsylvania. A devotee of the spiritual teacher, Ammachi, she was the one with Bob when he died. Rob and I were home resting. I know Bob chose to go then. But in the three days prior, a few old friends visited him. There is always a rally at the end and Bob was no exception. He wanted to be taken back to the hospital instead of remaining in hospice care. His physician and I had agreed to this and it was planned to move him the following Monday.

He died that Sunday night. Laurie fed him tiny bites of a Hershey's Kiss as communion. I am sure her prayers knocked on heaven's door and it opened to see him in. My friend John said he saw Bob rise straight into white light.

All I have left of those four days is a leaf that blew into his room. "The French doors flew open twice," Laurie said, "and the leaf blew in and landed at the foot of the bed, as if spirit had come to get him." And it had. You can see a picture of the leaf on my website, but a life well lived cannot be scanned quite so easily.

He was buried right before a winter storm hit Memphis, Tennessee, where the services were held. The cemetery was starkly beautiful as they laid him to rest. His journey will illuminate those who follow a path with heart. I know he is happy that I have chosen to continue on with my writing. Stay tuned—all is well.

> "There is a thread that must be followed
> carefully one step at a time
> until you reach the rocky crag
> then jump and reach your destination
> the mysterious moment when you rise."
> (Vicki Woodyard)

Mourning

Mourning has strong hands that wrestle me to the ground as I pit myself against it. I am no match for the darkness. Last night it was the walker my husband used as he grew sicker that made me weep for him the most. It made a certain sound as it carried him through the house from room to room. He was tall and the walker is bigger than most. It is beside the boxes of clothing that the Salvation Army will collect on Friday. Bits and pieces of a life going out the door.

Self-pity is not helpful, nor is it advisable. "Though He slay me, yet will I trust Him," says the Bible. It says nothing about my fear and anger, nor does it show a picture of my husband smiling through his horrific journey of the last five years. And now the rat has deserted the sinking ship and left me with all of the baggage. Bitterness expressed rather than suppressed. How could a loving husband kick me in the rear like this. He who guarded and protected me for a forty-year journey.

Yesterday I asked someone to replace the lock on my kitchen door. He just called and said that they no longer make that brand anymore. I will have to keep the one I have that is very hard to turn or replace the whole kit and caboodle on two doors. When Bob was sick, we had no time or energy for dealing with the small stuff like that. It's the small stuff that gets ya.

You Are What Bob Is

I told my friend Peter about Bob's death and this is his lovely reply:

"He is missed. It seems to me that what remains, of course, is love. His love for you and you for him. That always lasts. Life must have loved him dearly to take him into itself.

It seems that we are in a rowboat without oars, adrift on the river. What can we do? The current carries us, sometimes through smooth water, sometimes through rough. But it is all out of our control, no matter what we do, what we think, what we understand. So we go, carried we know not where, carried we know not how. Adrift under the clear bright stars, awed by the wide wild sky as we look up and see the stars shimmer and dance in their glory.

You are what Bob is."

Love, Peter

I was reading *My Grandfather's Blessings* by Rachel Naomi Remen. The words that came to me were, "Let us linger with the blessing. Let us linger with the reality of our suffering." Today I had lunch with my friend, Tallulah and she remarked that I was, in so many words, doing well. That is exactly the case and also not the case. For tonight brought soft tears and recollections of my husband's last days.

The blessing of his last days was this—that we saw with stark reality that he could no longer sustain the life spark in his sick body. That he was being called into the spirit world and we could not go with him. That shakes those who must remain behind. We knew the depth of our love for each other and yet the body was breaking quickly.

So now the bed is empty on his side and his dresser has a barren look as I stare at it. This loneliness is at least as real as the love we shared for so many years. I honor it exactly where it hits the hardest, in my heart. I let it strike me blind for a few moments, allow it to mute my voice and taste salt in my throat. It is appropriate for that to happen.

Does this mean that my life has been lessened in its blessings. No, not at all. For my wholeness calls out to me to dry my eyes and look again. Here is where I will live my life from now on. Here is how I will respond to the moment, just as I did before. Nothing has changed just because everything has changed. The emotional wrenching has left its scar and its blessing. The gift of love has never changed its course since the beginning; it runs totally through every vein of the soul, clear and free. It washes the eyes of sorrow clean and restores the lost moments of love. It is not finished; it has barely begun.

From A Mind Of Loss To A Heart Of Light

Writing this book was something I knew I would do when the time was right. Every step leading up to it was necessary. It has completed a cycle for me and a new vista opens up. I hear the silence now and see the peace of a perfectly ordinary day.

I continue to write and follow a spiritual practice of being myself. Bob knows I am a different *myself* than I used to be. I had a dream in which he came to me. He opened a journal and said to me, "Your prayers are written daily on the wall of my heart."

Someone once said that every prayer that goes out into the universe is actually answered deep within one's own heart. We are the outermost out and the innermost in. Nothing lies outside of the consciousness that we are.

So of course Bob is listening because there is no place that we are not. I want to end this book with something that will take your breath away. But I can't. Everything has been leading up to this moment and it is so...ordinary. I have gone up to the very gates of death and surrendered my loved one to the mystery. And I remain here rooted in being.

Julia Melges-Brenner did a reading for me about my path and she said this, in part.

"I see a tree now, and its branches grow naturally, always reaching up and out for the light. This is your path—to not shoot straight this way or that way, like an arrow, but to just keep reaching for the light, moment by moment, reaching out and reaching up, and in this way, blossoming beautifully."

That has become my journey clothed in words and light. I travel on, back to the place I never left.

In Days Of Great Peace

A devotee of Ramana Maharshi wrote a book with the title, *In Days of Great Peace*. His name was Mouni Sadhu. Since my husband's passing, I have begun to live in that space. How to say the ineffable? How to pronounce the words *I love you* to what has seemingly disappeared. It is unimportant in the face of everything that is.

There are words and candles and sentimentalities, but they are not That. The beloved has gone beyond and into the silence. The halls of the particular are wreathed with the universal, green and luxuriant with peace.

I have walked into the valley so often that even blinded by tears I know the way. This time I am walking it more consciously, carrying the light of the inner. Somehow it all falls into place as it falls apart again and again. Who knew that it would be like this?

> "The Body of B. Franklin, Printer
> Like the Cover of an old Book
> Its Contents turn out
> And Stript of its Lettering & Guilding ..."
> (from Ben Franklin's tombstone)

The body is no longer necessary, but the light that shone within it becomes even brighter.

ABOUT THE AUTHOR

Vicki Woodyard received a B.S. degree, *magna cum laude*, in English and Psychology from the University of Memphis. She was born in Memphis, Tennessee, and makes her home in Atlanta. She has spent her life on the spiritual path, her chief influence being Vernon Howard. Although Vicki has been writing all of her life, this is her first book.

CPSIA information can be obtained at www.ICGtesting.com
Printed in the USA
LVOW052315250712

291444LV00001B/150/P